TITLE:
UNSTOPPABLY RICH

SUBTITLE:
A FINANCIALLY FREE WOMAN'S GUIDE

BY

AMANDA B. JAMES

Copyright page

Table of Contents

Introduction

INTRODUCTION

Welcome to "UNSTOPPABLY RICH: A Financial Guide for Women."

In a world where women are breaking barriers, challenging norms, and achieving remarkable success in various fields, there's one arena where our potential is still vastly untapped—personal finance. This book is a powerful tool designed to empower you with the knowledge and confidence to take control of your financial future, regardless of where you are starting and what you have.

WHY THIS BOOK IS FOR YOU

Are you a woman who dreams of financial independence, but the world of money management seems overwhelming or out of reach? Perhaps you're well on your way, but you want to refine your financial strategy and strengthen your wealth-building skills. No matter your background or experience level, this book is tailored to meet you where you are and guide you towards financial empowerment.

"UNSTOPPABLY RICH" is not just another financial guide; it's a comprehensive resource crafted specifically for women, addressing the unique challenges and opportunities we face in today's financial landscape. Whether you're a recent graduate entering the workforce, a working professional aiming to negotiate that raise, a budding entrepreneur, or someone simply seeking financial peace of mind, this book has something valuable to offer.

HOW TO USE THIS GUIDE

This book is organized into nine chapters, each delving into a critical aspect of financial management. From setting and achieving your financial goals to investing wisely, navigating workplace dynamics, and building a strong support network, we cover it all. You can read this book sequentially or jump to specific chapters based on your needs and interests.

Throughout "UNSTOPPABLY RICH," you'll find practical advice, and actionable steps to help you make informed financial decisions. We'll demystify complex financial concepts, provide valuable tips, and offer strategies that can propel you toward financial success.

Remember, your journey to financial empowerment starts here, and you have the potential to become "UNSTOPPABLY RICH." Let's embark on this transformative journey together.

Are you ready to take control of your financial destiny and embrace a future filled with confidence and abundance? Let's begin!

CHAPTER ONE

SETTING YOUR FINANCIAL GOALS

DEFINING YOUR FINANCIAL VISION

The journey to financial empowerment begins with a clear vision of your financial future. In this chapter, we explore the importance of defining your financial goals and creating a vision that aligns with your aspirations, values, and dreams.

WHY GOALS MATTER

Financial goals provide direction and purpose to your financial decisions. They serve as a roadmap, helping you prioritize your spending, saving, and investing. Without clear goals, it's easy to drift aimlessly and miss out on opportunities to build wealth.

TYPES OF FINANCIAL GOALS

We discuss the distinction between short-term and long-term goals. Short-term goals might include paying off credit card debt or building an emergency fund, while long-term goals could involve retirement planning or buying a home. Understanding these categories allows you to set priorities and allocate resources effectively.

SETTING SMART GOALS

We introduce the SMART goal framework (Specific, Measurable, Achievable, Relevant, and Time-bound) as a powerful tool for goal setting. This framework helps you transform vague aspirations into concrete, actionable objectives. We provide practical exercises to help you create SMART financial goals tailored to your unique circumstances.

SHORT-TERM vs LONG-TERM GOALS

This section delves into the differences between short-term and long-term financial goals, emphasizing their coexistence in a balanced financial plan.

Long-term goals are objectives that you want to achieve over an extended period, often several years or even a lifetime. They provide a sense of direction and purpose in life, helping you plan for the future. Examples might include career aspirations, personal development, or financial independence.

Short-term goals, on the other hand, are more immediate and typically span days, weeks, or a few months. They serve as stepping stones toward your long-term goals, breaking them down into manageable tasks. Short-term goals are essential for maintaining focus and measuring progress.

Both long-term and short-term goals are crucial for personal growth and success, as they help you prioritize, stay motivated, and track your accomplishments along the way. Balancing these two types of goals is key to a well-rounded and purposeful life.

SHORT-TERM GOALS

We discuss the importance of short-term goals for immediate financial stability and peace of mind.

Tips for prioritizing short-term goals and developing strategies to achieve them.
Examples of common short-term goals such as paying off high-interest debt, creating an emergency fund, or funding a vacation.

BUDGETING AND EXPENSE MANAGEMENT

Short-term financial goals often involve creating and sticking to a budget. This can help you track your income and expenses, ensuring that you are living within your means and not overspending.

EMERGENCY FUND

One common short-term financial goal is to establish an emergency fund. Having savings set aside for unexpected expenses like medical bills or car repairs provides a financial safety net, reducing stress during emergencies.

DEBT REDUCTION

Short-term goals can focus on paying off high-interest debts. Reducing or eliminating credit card debt, for instance, can free up money for other immediate needs and reduce long-term financial burdens.

BUILDING FINANCIAL DISCIPLINE

Achieving short-term goals requires discipline and financial responsibility. Developing these habits can have a positive impact on your overall financial well-being.

REDUCING FINANCIAL STRESS

Meeting short-term financial goals can alleviate day-to-day financial stress. When you have a plan and are actively working towards financial objectives, you're less likely to worry about immediate financial needs.

SETTING PRIORITIES

Short-term goals help you prioritize your financial needs and wants. This can lead to better decision-making when it comes to spending and saving, ensuring that you allocate resources where they are most needed.

IMMEDIATE REWARDS

Achieving short-term goals provides a sense of accomplishment and instant gratification. This can boost your motivation to continue making financially responsible choices.

FLEXIBILITY

Short-term goals can be adjusted more easily than long-term goals. If your financial situation changes unexpectedly, you can adapt your short-term goals to fit your new circumstances.

LONG-TERM GOALS

A focus on the significance of long-term goals in securing your financial future and achieving major milestones.
Strategies for setting and funding long-term goals, including retirement planning and investments.
The power of compounding and time in growing wealth over the long run.

FINANCIAL SECURITY

Long-term goals, such as retirement planning and saving for major life events like buying a home or sending children to college, provide financial security as they ensure you have the resources to meet these needs when the time comes.

WEALTH ACCUMULATION

Long-term goals enable you to accumulate wealth over time through disciplined saving and investment. They allow you to harness the power of compound interest to grow your assets.

RETIREMENT PLANNING

Long-term goals, especially retirement planning, are critical for maintaining your quality of life in later years when you may no longer earn a regular income. They ensure you have the funds needed to enjoy a comfortable retirement.

ACHIEVING MILESTONES

Long-term goals serve as a roadmap to achieving major life milestones, such as buying a home, starting a business, or traveling the world. They provide direction and motivation to work steadily towards these objectives.

STRATEGIES FOR SETTING AND FUNDING LONG-TERM GOALS,INCLUDING RETIREMENT PLANNING AND INVESTMENTS:

GOAL CLARITY

Clearly define your long-term financial goals, including the amount of money required and the timeline for achieving them.

BUDGETING

Create a budget that allocates a portion of your income towards your long-term goals. Treat this allocation as a non-negotiable expense.

AUTOMATIC SAVING

Set up automatic transfers to a dedicated savings or investment account to ensure consistent contributions to your long-term goals.

REGULAR REVIEW

Periodically review your progress toward your long-term goals and adjust your strategies as needed. Life circumstances and financial markets can change, so flexibility is important.

THE POWER OF COMPOUNDING AND TIME IN GROWING WEALTH OVER THE LONG RUN

COMPOUND INTEREST

Compound interest is the concept where your earnings generate additional earnings. Over time, this snowball effect can significantly increase your wealth.

TIME HORIZON

The longer you invest and allow your investments to compound, the greater the impact on your wealth. Time is a valuable asset in wealth accumulation.

CONSISTENCY

Regular contributions and reinvesting earnings compound the growth of your investments. Consistency in saving and investing is key to reaping the full benefits of compounding.

In summary, long-term financial goals are instrumental in securing your financial future, achieving major life milestones, and accumulating wealth. To succeed in funding these goals, it's essential to set clear objectives, budget effectively, apply smart investment strategies, and understand the power of compound interest and the importance of time in growing your wealth.

SMART GOAL SETTING

Smart goal setting guides you through the process of creating SMART financial goals.

BE SPECIFIC

How to define your financial goals with precision, leaving no room for ambiguity.
Crafting clear and concise statements of what you want to achieve.

Instead of vague goals like "save money" or "get out of debt," be specific about what you want to accomplish. For example, "Save $10,000 for a down payment on a house" or "Pay off $5,000 in credit card debt."

MEASURABLE

Take note of this things in your journey to becoming financially independent as a woman:

1) The importance of quantifying your goals to track progress.

2) Techniques for measuring your financial success against predetermined benchmarks.

QUANTIFY YOUR GOALS

Attach a numerical value to your goals wherever possible. This helps you track progress and know when you've achieved your objectives.

SET A TIMELINE

Establish a realistic timeframe for achieving each goal. For instance, "Pay off $5,000 in credit card debt within 18 months."

PRIORITIZE

Determine which goals are most important to you. Some goals, like retirement savings or emergency funds, might take precedence over others.

ACHIEVABLE

1)Setting realistic goals that are within your reach.

2)Avoiding overambitious objectives that can lead to frustration and disappointment.

CONSIDER WHY

Understand the reasons behind your goals. Knowing why you want to achieve something can provide motivation and help you stay committed.

RELEVANT

1)Aligning your financial goals with your values and long-term vision.

2)Ensuring your goals have personal significance.

BREAK DOWN LARGER GOALS

 If you have big, long-term goals, break them into smaller, manageable steps. For instance, if your goal is to save $1 million for retirement, start with smaller annual savings targets.

WRITE IT DOWN

Document your goals in writing. This makes them more tangible and serves as a reminder of what you're working toward.

REVIEW AND ADJUST

Regularly review your goals to track progress and make any necessary adjustments. Life circumstances change, and your goals may need to evolve with them.

Always remember to apply the SMART (Specific, Measurable, Achievable, Relevant, Time-bound) criteria to your goals to ensure they meet these standards. SMART goals are inherently precise and actionable.

VISUALIZE SUCCESS

Create a mental picture of what achieving your goals will look and feel like. Visualization can enhance your motivation and focus.
Here's an example of a well-defined financial goal: "I will save $15,000 for a family vacation to Europe in three years by setting aside $500 per month in a dedicated savings account."

By following these steps and crafting precise statements for your financial goals, you eliminate ambiguity and create a clear path to achieving your aspirations. This clarity enhances your ability to plan, budget, and stay committed to your financial objectives.

TIME-BOUND

1)Setting deadlines for achieving your goals.

2)The role of time constraints in maintaining motivation and accountability.

By applying all that have been listed and explained in this whole chapter. You'll understand the importance of setting clear and achievable financial goals using the SMART framework. With your vision clarified, you'll be ready to move forward, equipped with a roadmap to financial empowerment.

Now let us go into constructing a solid financial foundation using practical knowledge in chapter 2.

CHAPTER TWO

BUILDING A SOLID FINANCIAL FOUNDATION

By the end of Chapter 2, you will have established a solid financial foundation. You'll learn the importance of budgeting, have the tools to create a budget based on your goals, and learn how to build and maintain an emergency fund. Plus, you'll develop strategies for debt management and reduction to help you on your way to financial security and success.

INTRODUCTION

Before embarking on your journey to financial empowerment, it is crucial to establish a solid foundation. This chapter focuses on the basic components of personal finance. Just as a stable building needs a solid foundation, your financial future depends on a solid foundation, including budgeting, emergency funds, and smart debt management.

BUDGETING 101

THE IMPORTANCE OF BUDGETING

Budgeting is the cornerstone of financial success. It's not about restriction, it's about awareness and control. Budgeting helps you to spend wisely and avoid bankruptcy,it is the springboard to financial advancement. In this section, we'll explore why budgeting is essential.

FINANCIAL AWARENESS

Budgeting helps you understand where your money goes and identifies areas for improvement. It also helps you to curb extravagant and unnecessary expenses.

CONTROL

It puts you in charge of your finances, allowing you to prioritize your goals instead of spending on impulse.

REDUCING STRESS

A well-structured budget can help to reduce financial stress by ensuring you have funds for important things and goals. Especially for emergency situations.

HOW TO CREATE A BUDGET

We break down the budgeting process into actionable steps:

INCOME ASSESSMENT

Calculate your total income, including regular paychecks and any other sources of income. Adequate calculation helps you plan ahead of time.

EXPENSES EVALUATION

Categorize your expenses into essentials like (housing, food, utilities) and non-essentials like (entertainment, dining out). You don't need to spend on things that are not very necessary.

SETTING PRIORITIES

Allocate funds to different expense categories based on your goals and needs. Learning how to set your priorities will help you not to mismanage your finance.

TRACKING SPENDING

Implement tools and methods to track your spending, such as apps or spreadsheets. Draft a todo list that will help you keep track of achievable goals.

ADJUSTMENTS

Periodically review and adjust your budget to accommodate changing circumstances. Proper adjustments will help you to keep your spending in check, you will not have to spend more than you earn or incur avoidable debts.

EMERGENCY FUND ESSENTIALS

What Is an Emergency Fund?
An emergency fund is your financial safety net, providing peace of mind when unexpected expenses arise. We discuss:

Why You Need One:

Emergencies happen to everyone, and an emergency fund ensures you're prepared for them.

How Much to Save:

Guidelines for determining the appropriate size of your emergency fund. Sometimes how much you earn can play a vital role in determining the size of your emergency fund,learn to draft reasonable guides that is geared toward appropriate saving.

Where to Keep It:

Tips for keeping your emergency fund accessible yet separate from your regular spending accounts. Know useful tips that will help you keep your emergency fund safe and secure.

Building Your Emergency Fund:

You should learn to provide strategies to build or replenish your emergency fund, even if you're on a tight budget.

This includes:

Automated Savings:

Setting up automatic transfers to your emergency fund will help you to stay on track. Automated fund transfer can be weekly or monthly,depending on your level of income.

Cutting Unnecessary Expenses:

Identifying areas where you can trim spending to redirect funds toward your fund. Placing your priorities right is a springboard to proper fund management, you don't spend on just anything because you fancy it.

Windfalls and Bonuses:

Maximizing unexpected financial windfalls, such as tax refunds or bonuses.

Managing Debt Wisely:

Understanding Debt
Debt is a double-edged sword. When managed wisely, it can be a tool for financial growth. Mismanaged, it can lead to a cycle of financial stress. Implementing good debt management policies can help you to eliminate poor managerial skill.

We cover:

Types of Debt:

Understanding the difference between good debt (investments like mortgages or student loans) and bad debt (high-interest credit card debt).

Interest Rates:

Always try to evaluate and compare interest rates on loans and credit cards. Just because you need money to sort out your financial needs doesn't mean you should incur unreasonable amount of debts, take time to check and compare interest rates before you go ahead to take a loan, some debts can destabilize you, you might not even see it coming until you are fully committed.

Strategies for Managing Debt:

Some actionable strategies for managing and reducing debt, includes:

Debt Repayment Plans:

 Creating a structured plan for paying down debt. Don't just wait till it's due time to repay your debts, always be in control of your funds as that will help you strategize on how to make a repayment even before the time is due.

Debt Consolidation:

Strategize on how to consolidate high-interest debt into more manageable forms.

Avoiding New Debt:

Always look for tips for preventing further debt accumulation. Channel your loans to profitable things that are capable of settling the interest rate. Ensure not to spend the money on frivolous things or activities.

By implementing everything you have learnt from this chapter, you will comfortably establish a solid financial foundation. You'll understand the importance of budgeting, have the tools to create a budget tailored to your goals, and know how to build and maintain an emergency fund. Additionally, you'll have strategies for managing and reducing debt, setting you on the path to financial security and success.

CHAPTER THREE

INVESTING FOR YOUR FUTURE

INTRODUCTION:

Investing is a powerful tool for building wealth over time. In this chapter, we'll explore the world of investments and how you can leverage them to secure your financial future. Whether you're just starting or looking to expand your investment portfolio, understanding the basics is crucial.

INVESTMENT BASICS

THE IMPORTANCE OF INVESTING

Investing allows your money to work for you. We discuss:

Building Wealth: investments can grow your money over time through compound interest. Investing allows you to grow your wealth over time by earning returns on your investments, such as stocks, bonds, real estate, or businesses.

Beating Inflation: The role of investments in outpacing the erosion of purchasing power due to inflation. Money left idle loses value due to inflation. Investing can potentially outpace inflation, preserving the purchasing power of your money.

Financial Independence: Investing can help you achieve long-term financial goals, such as retirement. Investing helps you secure your financial future, providing a source of income and assets for retirement or unexpected expenses.

Passive Income: Investments like stocks and real estate can generate passive income through dividends, rental income, or interest payments.

Diversification: Investing in a variety of assets spreads risk and reduces the impact of a downturn in any one investment.

Retirement Planning: Investing in retirement accounts like IRAs helps you build a nest egg for your retirement years.

Achieving Financial Goals: Investing can help you reach specific financial goals, such as buying a house, funding education, or starting a business.

Tax Benefits: Certain investments come with tax advantages, like tax-deferred growth or tax deductions, which can reduce your overall tax liability.

Economic Growth: Investing in businesses and infrastructure contributes to economic growth and job creation, benefiting society as a whole.

Compound Growth: Over time, investments can benefit from compounding, where your earnings generate more earnings, accelerating your wealth accumulation.

Types of Investments
We introduce various investment options, including:

Stocks: Ownership in a company, offering the potential for high returns but with higher risk.

Bonds: Loans to governments or corporations with predictable interest payments.

Real Estate: Investing in physical properties for rental income or capital appreciation.

Mutual Funds and ETFs: Diversified portfolios of stocks and bonds managed by professionals.

Retirement Accounts: Tax-advantaged accounts like 401(k)s and IRAs for long-term savings.

RISK TOLERANCE AND DIVERSIFICATION

Understanding your risk tolerance is key to creating a balanced investment portfolio.
An individual's risk tolerance plays a crucial role in determining the appropriate mix of investments.
Your willingness and ability to tolerate risk should align with your financial goals, time horizon, and comfort level with potential losses.

DIVERSIFICATION:

Investors often aim to strike a balance between risk and potential return by diversifying their portfolios. Diversification involves spreading investments across different asset classes (e.g., stocks, bonds, real estate) to reduce overall risk while still seeking reasonable returns.

RISK vs REWARD

The relationship between risk and potential return in investments.

Higher Risk, Higher Potential Return:

In general, investments with higher levels of risk have the potential for higher returns. Riskier investments typically involve more uncertainty and volatility, which can lead to greater profit opportunities. For example, stocks of emerging companies or industries might have the potential for substantial gains but also carry higher risk.

Lower Risk, Lower Potential Return:

Conversely, investments with lower risk tend to offer lower potential returns. Safer investments, such as government bonds or savings accounts, are typically more stable and have less potential for substantial growth compared to riskier assets.

Risk Assessment:

Always look for tools and ask questions to help you determine your risk tolerance.

It is essential to note that investing also carries risks, and it's crucial to educate yourself, diversify your portfolio, and consider your risk tolerance before making investment decisions. Consulting with a financial advisor can also be beneficial. As we go further to explore chapter 3, we will discuss comprehensively how to navigate the workplace while balancing your finances and moving unstoppably.

CHAPTER FOUR

NAVIGATING THE WORKPLACE

NEGOTIATING YOUR SALARY

KNOW YOUR WORTH:

RESEARCHING SALARY RANGES FOR YOUR POSITION AND INDUSTRY:

Researching salary ranges for your position and industry is essential for making informed career decisions. Start by using online resources like salary websites or industry-specific surveys to gather data on typical compensation. Consider factors like location, experience, and education when assessing salary ranges. Networking with professionals in your field can also provide valuable insights. Ultimately, this research will help you negotiate fair compensation and set realistic career goals.

EFFECTIVE NEGOTIATIONS: Make sure you use effective strategies and tips for successful salary negotiations.

RESEARCH: Know your market value by researching industry standards and salary ranges for your position.

SET CLEAR EXPECTATIONS: Define your desired salary and benefits in advance to have a clear goal.

HIGHLIGHT YOUR VALUE: During the discussion, emphasize your skills, experience, and achievements that make you an asset to the company.

LISTEN ACTIVELY: Understand the employer's perspective and be open to compromises.

TIMING: Choose the right moment for negotiation, often after a job offer but before accepting.

STAY PROFESSIONAL: Maintain a polite and respectful tone, even if negotiations become challenging.

PRACTICE: Role-play with a friend to improve your negotiation skills. This will help you to tackle real life difficulties that you will encounter during your negotiation.

CONSIDER NON-SALARY BENEFITS: Explore other perks like flexible hours, remote work options, or professional development opportunities.

BE PREPARED TO WALK AWAY: If the offer doesn't meet your needs, be ready to decline and continue your job search. Don't settle for a job that doesn't bring in the resources that you need to take care of expenses,your pay should be enough to cover for you time.

FOLLOW UP IN WRITING: After reaching an agreement, request a written offer to avoid misunderstandings.

Remember, successful negotiation is a two-way street, aiming for a win-win outcome where both you and the employer are satisfied.

LONG-TERM IMPACT:

How negotiating a higher salary can significantly impact your lifetime earnings;

Negotiating a higher salary can have a profound long-term impact on your lifetime earnings. Even a modest increase can lead to substantial financial gains over time. When you secure a higher starting salary, future raises, bonuses, and retirement contributions are all based on this higher baseline. Over the course of your career, these compounding gains can add up to hundreds of thousands or even millions of dollars in additional income, which can significantly enhance your financial security and quality of life.

RETIREMENT PLANNING

The Power of Early Saving:

The benefits of starting to save for retirement as early as possible is vital.
The power of early saving for retirement is immense. When you start saving in your 20s or 30s, your money has more time to grow through compounding. Over the years, even small contributions can multiply into a substantial nest egg. Additionally, you'll be less reliant on riskier investments and have a financial safety net. Early saving means more flexibility and security in your retirement years, ensuring a comfortable and stress-free future.

RETIREMENT ACCOUNTS: An overview of different retirement accounts and their tax advantages.

1)401(k): Employer-sponsored plan with pre-tax contributions, potential employer match, and tax-deferred growth. You pay taxes when you withdraw in retirement.

2)Traditional IRA: Individual retirement account with pre-tax contributions, tax-deferred growth, and taxes paid upon withdrawal.

3)Roth IRA: Contributions are post-tax, but withdrawals are tax-free. Ideal for long-term tax-free growth.

4)SEP IRA and SIMPLE IRA: Geared towards self-employed individuals and small businesses, offering tax benefits for retirement savings.

5)HSA: While primarily for healthcare, it can also serve as a retirement account with triple tax benefits (tax-free contributions, growth, and withdrawals for qualified medical expenses).

Choosing the right account depends on your income, age, and retirement goals. Each has its own unique tax advantages, so it's wise to consult a financial advisor for personalized guidance.

EMPLOYER CONTRIBUTIONS: How to take advantage of employer-sponsored retirement plans.
BENEFITS AND PERKS

1)PARTICIPATION: Enroll as soon as you're eligible. Many employers offer matching contributions, which is essentially free money for your retirement.

2)CONTRIBUTE ENOUGH: Aim to contribute at least enough to receive the full employer match. This maximizes your savings.

3)AUTOMATIC CONTRIBUTIONS: Set up automatic deductions from your paycheck. It ensures consistency and discipline in saving.

4)DIVERSIFY INVESTMENTS: Choose a diversified portfolio within the plan that matches your risk tolerance and retirement goals.

5)TAKE ADVANTAGE OF TAX BENEFITS:
These plans often offer tax advantages, like tax-deferred growth. Understand how these benefits work in your favor.

6)REVIEW AND ADJUST: Periodically review your contributions and investment choices to make sure they align with your retirement objectives.

7)EDUCATE YOURSELF: Understand the plan's rules, investment options, and any investing schedules to make informed decisions.

Employer-sponsored retirement plans can significantly boost your retirement savings, so make the most of these benefits and perks to secure your financial future.

UNDERSTANDING BENEFITS: An overview of common workplace benefits like health insurance and paid time off:

1)HEALTH INSURANCE: This provides coverage for medical expenses, including doctor visits, hospital stays, and prescription drugs. Employers often share the cost.

2)PAID TIME OFF (PTO): This Includes vacation, sick leave, and holidays. PTO allows you to take paid time away from work to rest and recharge.

3)RETIREMENT PLANS: Employer-sponsored plans, like 401(k)s, help you save for retirement with potential employer contributions.

4)DENTAL AND VISION INSURANCE: These can be separate from regular health insurance and cover dental and eye care expenses.

5)LIFE INSURANCE: Provides financial security for your family in case of your death. Employers may offer a basic policy and the option to purchase additional coverage.

6)DISABILITY INSURANCE: Protects your income if you're unable to work due to illness or injury.

7)FLEXIBLE SPENDING ACCOUNTS (FSAs) AND HEALTH SAVINGS ACCOUNTS (HSAs): Allow you to set aside pre-tax dollars for medical expenses.

8)EMPLOYEE ASSISTANCE PROGRAMS (EAPs): Offer counseling and support services for various life challenges.

Understanding these benefits ensures you make the most of your workplace perks and maintain your well-being, both in the present and for the future.

MAXIMIZING BENEFITS: Tips for making the most of your employee benefits package.

1)EDUCATE YOURSELF: Understand every benefit offered, including eligibility requirements, coverage limits, and any associated costs.

2)CUSTOMIZE BENEFITS: Choose benefits that align with your needs. For example, if you have a family, comprehensive health insurance may be a priority.

3)CONTRIBUTE TO RETIREMENT: Contribute enough to your retirement plan to receive the full employer match. It's essentially free money.

4) USE TAX-ADVANTAGED ACCOUNTS: If available, use Flexible Spending Accounts (FSAs) and Health Savings Accounts (HSAs) to reduce your taxable income.

5) WELLNESS PROGRAMS: Take advantage of wellness initiatives, such as gym memberships or mental health support, to stay healthy and reduce healthcare costs.

BALANCING BENEFITS AND SALARY:Considering the total compensation package when evaluating job offers.

1)EVALUATE TOTAL COMPENSATION: Consider the value of your benefits package in addition to your salary. Sometimes, a lower salary with better benefits can result in higher overall compensation.

2) PRIORITIZE YOUR NEEDS: Different life stages may require different benefits. Consider what's most important to you and your family at any given time.

3) LONG-TERM FOCUS: Retirement contributions and health benefits can have a significant long-term impact. Think about how these benefits support your future financial security.

Balancing benefits and salary and maximizing your employee benefits package can lead to a more rewarding and financially secure work experience.

By now,you have achieved a solid understanding of investment fundamentals, including the types of investments available and how to manage risk through diversification. You'll also gain insights into the workplace dynamics, including salary negotiation, retirement planning, and maximizing employee benefits. Armed with this knowledge, you'll be better equipped to make informed financial decisions and work towards your financial goals.

CHAPTER FIVE

ENTREPRENEURSHIP AND SIDE HUSTLES

INTRODUCTION

Entrepreneurship and side hustles offer women unique opportunities to take control of their financial destinies. In this chapter, we delve into the world of entrepreneurship and explore how to successfully launch and manage a side hustle while maintaining financial stability.

EXPLORING ENTREPRENEURSHIP

THE ENTREPRENEURIAL MINDSET

Risk-Taking: Discussing the willingness to take calculated risks as a key trait of successful entrepreneurs.

The entrepreneurial mindset often centers around a willingness to take calculated risks. Successful entrepreneurs understand that risk is inherent in business but can be managed intelligently. They:

1)ASSESS OPPORTUNITIES: Identify potential opportunities by weighing potential rewards against risks. This analysis informs decision-making.

2) EMBRACING UNCERTAINTY: Entrepreneurs accept that uncertainty is part of the journey. They

use it as a driving force for innovation and adaptability.

3) LEARN FROM FAILURE: Recognize that some risks may not pan out, but failures provide valuable lessons for future endeavors.

4) STAY RESILIENT: Even when facing setbacks, successful entrepreneurs remain resilient, adjusting their strategies and pushing forward.

5) SEEK EXPERTISE: They seek advice and expertise to minimize risks and make informed decisions.

In the entrepreneurial world, taking calculated risks is a key trait that can lead to innovation, growth, and success.

CREATIVITY AND INNOVATION: How thinking outside the box can lead to business opportunities.

Creativity and innovation are catalysts for business opportunities. When individuals and organizations think outside the box:

1)IDENTIFYING UNMET NEEDS: Creativity helps in spotting unmet needs or problems, providing a foundation for unique solutions.

2) COMPETITIVE ADVANTAGE: Innovative ideas can set a business apart from competitors, attracting customers seeking fresh, distinctive offerings.

3) ADAPTING TO CHANGE: In rapidly evolving markets, creative thinking enables businesses to adapt and stay relevant.

4) COST EFFICIENCY: Innovations can streamline processes, reduce costs, and enhance productivity, improving the bottom line.

5) NEW MARKETS: Creative ideas often open doors to new markets, expanding the customer base and satisfaction.

By fostering a culture of creativity and innovation, businesses can tap into a wealth of opportunities and remain agile in an ever-changing world.

RESILIENCE: Dealing with setbacks and challenges as part of the entrepreneurial journey.

Resilience is a crucial trait for entrepreneurs as setbacks and challenges are inevitable on the entrepreneurial journey. It involves:

1)ADAPTABILITY: Being open to change and quick to adjust strategies when faced with unexpected obstacles.

2) PROBLEM-SOLVING: Viewing setbacks as opportunities to learn and solve problems, leading to growth and improvement.

3) PERSISTENCE: Maintaining the determination to continue despite adversity, often leading to breakthroughs and success. Persistence breaks resistance.

4) MENTAL TOUGHNESS: Developing the emotional fortitude to handle stress and uncertainty without losing focus.

5)NETWORKING: Leveraging relationships and support systems to gain insights and resources when facing challenges.

Resilience is not just about bouncing back but also about bouncing forward, using setbacks as springboards to greater achievements.

IDENTIFYING BUSINESS OPPORTUNITIES

Market Research: The importance of researching your target market and understanding customer needs.

Identifying business opportunities starts with comprehensive market research, which involves:

1)UNDERSTANDING CUSTOMER NEEDS:
Recognizing the problems or needs of your potential customers and how your product or service can address them is vital for every business.

2) MARKET ASSESSMENT: Evaluating the size of the market, its growth potential, and any gaps or underserved segments is one of the major factors that promotes a business.

3) COMPETITOR ANALYSIS: Studying existing competitors to identify their strengths and weaknesses and find ways to differentiate your offering can boost your business.

4) TRENDS AND INSIGHTS: Keeping an eye on industry trends, consumer behavior, and emerging technologies to spot opportunities for innovation.

5) VALIDATION: Testing your business idea with potential customers to gather feedback and refine your concept can help you make positive changes that will affect your business in the best way.

Thorough market research is the foundation for spotting viable business opportunities and increasing the chances of success in a competitive market.

YOUR PASSION AND SKILLS: How to align your business ideas with your passions and expertise.

Aligning your business ideas with your passions and skills is a smart strategy for success:

1)IDENTIFY YOUR PASSIONS: Reflect on what genuinely excites you and brings you joy. This passion can be a powerful motivator in building and sustaining a business.

2) ASSESS YOUR SKILLS: Recognize your strengths, expertise, and areas where you excel. Leverage these skills to add value to your business.

3) FIND OVERLAPS: Look for areas where your passions and skills intersect. This is where you're most likely to excel and enjoy the entrepreneurial journey.

4) MARKET DEMAND: Ensure there's a market need for the product or service that aligns with your passion and skills. A viable business idea should meet customer demand.

5) CONTINUOUS LEARNING: Be open to continuous learning and skill development to grow your business effectively.

Aligning passion and skills with your business ideas not only makes the journey more fulfilling but also increases your chances of long-term success.

 PROBLEM SOLVING: Identifying problems that your business can solve.
Balancing Your Side Hustle

Successful businesses often begin by identifying and solving problems to balancing your side hustle:

1)PROBLEM IDENTIFICATION: Recognize the pain points or unmet needs in your target market that your side hustle can address. This ensures a clear value proposition.

2) MARKET VALIDATION: Verify that there's a demand for the solution you're offering by conducting research or testing your idea with potential customers.

3) EFFECTIVE COMMUNICATION: Clearly communicate how your side hustle solves these problems. Your marketing and messaging should highlight the value you provide.

4) ADAPTABILITY: Be willing to adjust your offerings as you discover new challenges or opportunities in your market.

Identifying and solving real problems is the foundation for a successful side hustle that can potentially grow into a full-fledged business.

SIDE HUSTLE vs. FULL-TIME ENTREPRENEURSHIP

SIDE HUSTLE: This involves pursuing a business or income-generating activity alongside a regular job. It's often less risky, allows for steady income, and can be a testing ground for business ideas.

FULL-TIME ENTREPRENEURSHIP: Here, you commit all your time and resources to your business venture. It can be riskier, with the potential for higher rewards, but it requires a more significant initial investment and a willingness to take on financial uncertainty.
The choice between a side hustle and full-time entrepreneurship depends on your financial situation, risk tolerance, and the readiness of your business concept. Many successful entrepreneurs begin with a side hustle before transitioning to full-time when their venture becomes sustainable.

PROS AND CONS: WEIGHING THE BENEFITS AND DRAWBACKS OF STARTING A SIDE HUSTLE VERSUS A FULL-TIME BUSINESS

SIDE HUSTLE

PROS:

LOW RISK: Minimal financial risk, as you can maintain a stable income from a full-time job.
Skill Development: Opportunity to build skills and test business concepts with lower pressure.

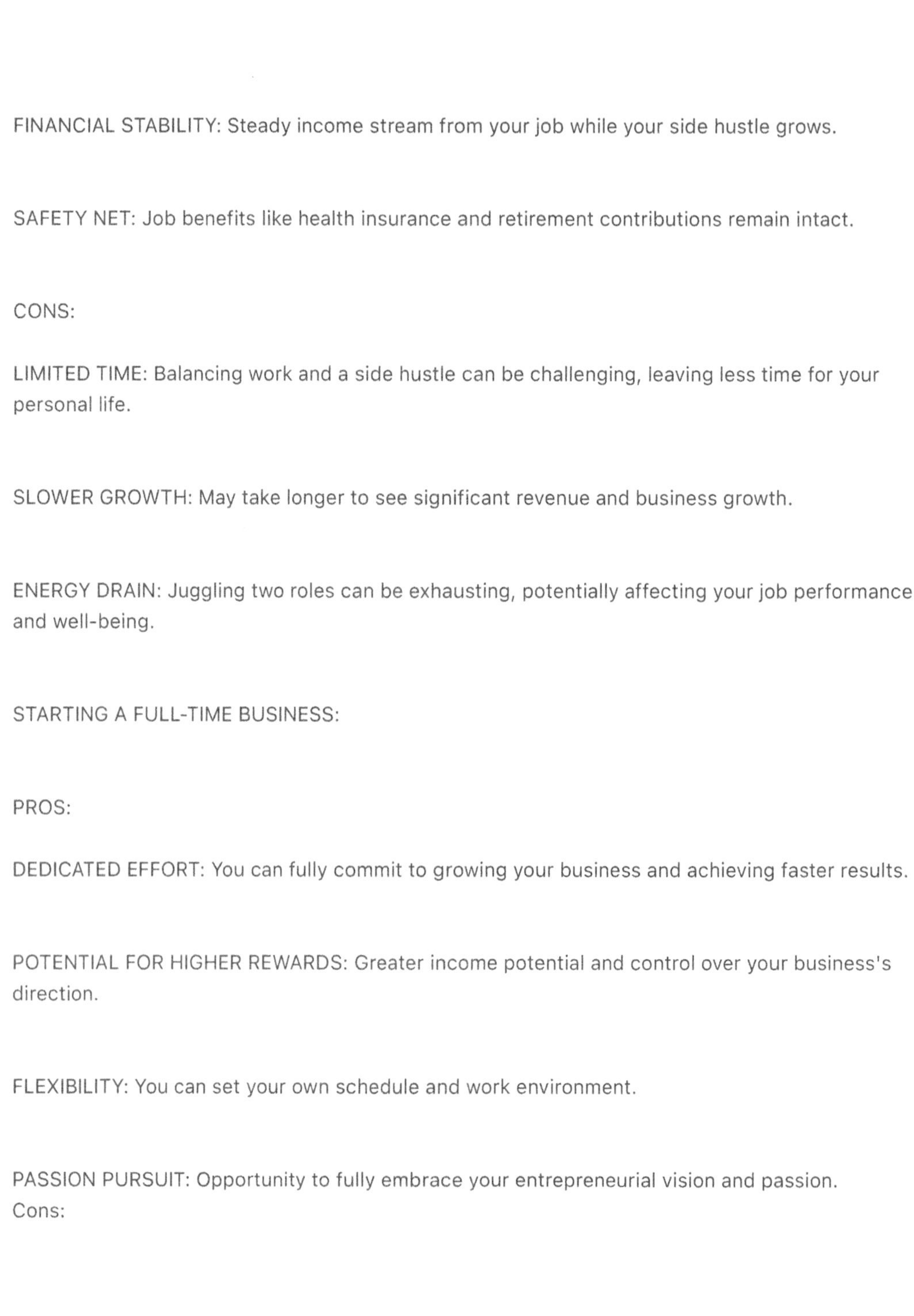

FINANCIAL STABILITY: Steady income stream from your job while your side hustle grows.

SAFETY NET: Job benefits like health insurance and retirement contributions remain intact.

CONS:

LIMITED TIME: Balancing work and a side hustle can be challenging, leaving less time for your personal life.

SLOWER GROWTH: May take longer to see significant revenue and business growth.

ENERGY DRAIN: Juggling two roles can be exhausting, potentially affecting your job performance and well-being.

STARTING A FULL-TIME BUSINESS:

PROS:

DEDICATED EFFORT: You can fully commit to growing your business and achieving faster results.

POTENTIAL FOR HIGHER REWARDS: Greater income potential and control over your business's direction.

FLEXIBILITY: You can set your own schedule and work environment.

PASSION PURSUIT: Opportunity to fully embrace your entrepreneurial vision and passion.
Cons:

FINANCIAL RISK: Higher financial risk as you may lack a stable income source during the initial stages.

STRESS: Increased stress due to financial uncertainty and the responsibility of running a business.

RESOURCE INTENSIVE: Requires substantial time and effort, often with limited personal time.

The choice between a side hustle and full-time business depends on your risk tolerance, financial situation, and commitment level. Many entrepreneurs begin with a side hustle and transition to full-time entrepreneurship when the business is more established.

TRANSITIONING STRATEGIES:
TIPS FOR TRANSITIONING FROM A SIDE HUSTLE TO A FULL-TIME BUSINESS IF THAT'S YOUR GOAL AND MANAGING YOUR TIME AND ENERGY.

Transitioning from a side hustle to a full-time business is a significant step. Here are some tips for a smooth transition:

1)FINANCIAL PREPARATION: Save enough to cover living expenses for several months, as your business may not generate immediate income.

2) BUSINESS PLAN: Create a solid business plan that outlines your vision, target market, and financial projections. This plan will guide your transition.

3) BUILD A SAFETY NET: Ensure you have a financial safety net or access to emergency funds for unexpected expenses.

4) SCALE GRADUALLY: If possible, gradually increase your commitment to the business, reducing

hours at your job as your business grows.

5) NETWORKING: Build a strong network of mentors and contacts who can provide guidance and support during your transition.

6) TIME MANAGEMENT: Be diligent about time management to balance work, personal life, and your business effectively.

7) HEALTH AND WELL-BEING: Prioritize self-care to maintain your physical and mental well-being during this transition.
Moving from a side hustle to a full-time business can be challenging, but with careful planning and commitment, it's a rewarding step toward pursuing your entrepreneurial dreams.

AVOIDING BURNOUTS: Tips for maintaining a healthy work-life balance.

Avoiding burnout is essential for maintaining a healthy work-life balance:

1)SET BOUNDARIES: Define clear work hours and personal time, and stick to them as closely as possible.

2) PRIORITIZE SELF-CARE: Make time for relaxation, exercise, and activities you enjoy outside of work.

3) DELEGATE AND SEEK HELP: Don't hesitate to delegate tasks or ask for support when needed, both at work and in your personal life.

4) LEARN TO SAY NO: Avoid overcommitting by politely declining tasks or responsibilities that you can't manage.

5) TAKE BREAKS: Incorporate short breaks throughout your workday to recharge and refocus.

6) UNPLUG: Disconnect from work-related devices and emails during your personal time to avoid constant work-related stress.

7) TIME MANAGEMENT: Use effective time management techniques to prioritize tasks and reduce time wasted on unproductive activities.

Balancing work and personal life is crucial for your well-being and long-term productivity. Remember that a healthy work-life balance benefits both your personal life and your professional success. Don't spend your health gaining wealth!

PRIORITIZATION: Identifying the most critical tasks in your side hustle to maximize productivity.

Prioritization is key for maximizing productivity in your side hustle:

1) URGENCY AND IMPORTANCE: Use the Eisenhower Matrix to categorize tasks as urgent/important, not urgent/important, urgent/not important, or neither. Focus on the urgent/important tasks first.

2) GOAL ALIGNMENT: Ensure that your tasks align with your business goals and long-term vision. Concentrate on activities that directly contribute to your success.

3) TIME SENSITIVITY: Consider deadlines and time-sensitive tasks. Tackle those that have impending due dates.

4) IMPACT: Assess the potential impact of each task on your business. Prioritize those with the highest potential for positive outcomes.

5) EFFICIENCY: Evaluate how efficiently you can complete a task. Sometimes quick wins can make a big difference.

By prioritizing effectively, you can concentrate your efforts on what truly matters, boosting productivity and achieving your side hustle goals more efficiently.

TAX CONSIDERATIONS & UNDERSTANDING TAXES

Understanding tax considerations is crucial for individuals and businesses to ensure legal compliance and minimize tax liabilities. Here's a comprehensive overview:

1. TYPES IF TAXES:

Income Tax: Levied on an individual's or business's earnings, both at the federal and state levels. The rate is often progressive, meaning higher income is taxed at a higher rate.

Sales Tax: Collected on the sale of goods and, in some cases, services. Rates and rules vary by state or region.

Property Tax: Based on the assessed value of real estate and is typically collected by local governments to fund schools, infrastructure, and other public services.

Corporate Tax: A tax on the profits of businesses, typically at both federal and state levels.

2. TAX PLANNING:

Deductions and Credits: Individuals and businesses can take advantage of deductions and credits to reduce their taxable income and liability. Common deductions include mortgage interest, student loan interest, and business expenses.

Tax-Efficient Investments: Investors can choose investments that offer tax advantages, such as tax-free municipal bonds or retirement accounts like IRAs and 401(k)s.

Timing of Income and Expenses: Tax planning can involve deferring income or accelerating expenses to reduce the current tax liability.

3. RECORD-KEEPING:

Maintain Accurate Records: Keep thorough records of income, expenses, and deductions, whether you're an individual or a business. This documentation is essential for tax filing and potential audits.

4. COMPLIANCE:

Filing Requirements: Understand your obligations for filing tax returns. Individuals typically file annually, while businesses may have different schedules.

Payment Deadlines: Be aware of deadlines for tax payments, as late payments can result in penalties and interest charges.

5. TAX SOFTWARE AND PROFESSIONALS:

Tax Software: Utilize tax preparation software or online services to help with tax calculations and filing. They can streamline the process and help identify deductions.

Tax Professionals: For complex tax situations, consider hiring a certified public accountant (CPA) or tax attorney to provide expert advice and assistance.

6. CHANGES IN TAX LAWS:

Stay informed about changes in tax laws, as they can significantly impact your tax liability. This includes keeping up with federal and state tax codes and regulations.

7.INTERNATIONAL TAX CONSIDERATIONS:

If you're involved in international business or have assets abroad, understanding international tax laws, treaties, and compliance is crucial.

8. ESTATE AND INHERITANCE TAX:

Estate and inheritance taxes apply to the transfer of wealth after an individual's death. Understanding these taxes is important for estate planning.

In summary, understanding taxes and making informed decisions regarding tax planning, compliance, and record-keeping can help individuals and businesses manage their tax liabilities effectively and legally. Consulting with a tax professional is often advisable for complex tax situations.

BUSINESS STRUCTURES: An overview of different business structures and their tax implications (e.g., sole proprietorship, LLC, corporation).

Different business structures have varying tax implications. Here's a brief overview:

SOLE PROPRIETORSHIP:

Tax Simplicity: Business income and expenses are reported on the owner's personal tax return (Form 1040).

Self-Employment Tax: Owners are responsible for self-employment taxes, covering both the employee and employer portions of Social Security and Medicare taxes.

Limited Liability Company (LLC):
Pass-Through Taxation: LLCs often have pass-through taxation, where business profits and losses flow through to the owner's personal tax return.

Self-Employment Tax: Owners may be subject to self-employment taxes unless they elect corporate tax treatment.

PARTNERSHIP:

Pass-Through Taxation: Similar to LLCs, partnership income and expenses pass through to the partners' personal tax returns.
Self-Employment Tax: Partners are typically subject to self-employment taxes.

C-CORPORATION:

Double Taxation: C-corps face double taxation, meaning the corporation pays taxes on profits, and shareholders pay taxes on dividends received.

Corporate Tax Rates: C-corps have their tax rates, which may be lower or higher than individual rates.

S-CORPORATION:

Pass-Through Taxation: S-corps offer pass-through taxation, like partnerships and LLCs, avoiding double taxation.

Salary vs. Distributions: Owners who work in the business typically take a reasonable salary, subject to payroll taxes, while the remainder can be distributed with lower tax liability.

NON PROFIT ORGANIZATION:

Tax-Exempt Status: If granted 501(c)(3) status, nonprofits are generally exempt from federal income tax.

Restrictions: Nonprofits have specific restrictions on income use and activities.
The choice of business structure can significantly impact your tax liability and other aspects of your business. It's crucial to consult with a tax professional or attorney to determine the most suitable structure based on your specific circumstances and goals.

TAX DEDUCTIONS: Identifying tax deductions and credits available to entrepreneurs and side hustlers.

Entrepreneurs and side hustlers can benefit from various tax deductions and credits to reduce their tax liabilities. Some common deductions and credits include:

HOME OFFICE DEDUCTION: If you use a portion of your home exclusively for your business, you can deduct related expenses like rent, utilities, and insurance.

BUSINESS EXPENSES: Deduct costs for supplies, equipment, marketing, and travel necessary for your business.

SELF-EMPLOYMENT TAX DEDUCTION: Self-employed individuals can deduct the employer portion of their Social Security and Medicare taxes.

HEALTH INSURANCE PREMIUMS: Entrepreneurs may deduct health insurance premiums for themselves and their dependents.

RETIREMENT CONTRIBUTIONS: Contributions to retirement plans like a SEP-IRA or Solo 401(k) are tax-deductible.

Qualified Business Income Deduction (QBI): This deduction can apply to eligible small business owners, reducing taxable income.
Research and Development Credits: Some entrepreneurs may qualify for tax credits related to research and development activities.

STARTUP COSTS: Deduct certain startup expenses incurred when launching a new business.

WORK OPPORTUNITY TAX CREDIT: Hiring certain employees, like veterans, can qualify you for tax credits.

EDUCATION AND TRAINING: Expenses for improving your skills and knowledge relevant to your business may be deductible.
It's essential to keep thorough records, consult a tax professional, and stay updated on tax laws to ensure you maximize these deductions and credits while staying compliant.

RECORD KEEPING: The importance of maintaining accurate financial records for tax purposes.

Maintaining accurate financial records is crucial for tax purposes for several reasons:

1)TAX COMPLIANCE: Proper records help ensure that you meet tax deadlines and comply with tax laws, reducing the risk of penalties or audits.

2) DEDUCTION ELIGIBILITY: Accurate records help identify eligible deductions and credits, minimizing your tax liability.

3) AUDIT DEFENSE: Detailed records provide evidence to support your tax return if you're audited by tax authorities.

4) FINANCIAL INSIGHTS: Well-kept records offer insights into your business's financial health and

performance, aiding in informed decision-making.

5) BUSINESS GROWTH: Clear financial records help secure financing and attract investors, supporting your business's growth.

6) REDUCED STRESS: Organized records make tax season less stressful, as you can quickly and confidently file your returns.

7) LEGAL REQUIREMENTS: Some business structures, like corporations, have legal obligations to maintain detailed financial records.

In summary, accurate record-keeping is essential for both tax compliance and overall financial management, benefiting your business in the long run.

This chapter is developed to give you a comprehensive understanding of entrepreneurship and side hustles and how to develop an entrepreneurial mindset, identifying business opportunities, and managing your time and energy effectively while balancing a side hustle. Additionally, you'll have insights into the tax considerations that come with entrepreneurship, ensuring you navigate your financial affairs in a compliant and advantageous manner. This knowledge will empower you to pursue your entrepreneurial dreams while maintaining financial stability and success.

CHAPTER SIX

WOMEN AND WEALTH

INTRODUCTION

In this chapter, we move into the critical topic of women and wealth. Despite significant progress, women still face unique financial challenges and opportunities. This chapter explores these dynamics and provides insights to help women overcome financial stereotypes, address the gender wage gap, and find inspiration from female wealth role models.

OVERCOMING FINANCIAL STEREOTYPES

Overcoming financial stereotypes is essential for fostering equality and promoting financial well-being. Here's how to address them:

EDUCATION: Promote financial literacy to empower individuals to make informed financial decisions regardless of their background.

CHALLENGE BIAS: Encourage open conversations about financial stereotypes and challenge assumptions or biases when they arise.

DIVERSE REPRESENTATION: Advocate for diversity and inclusion in finance-related fields to break stereotypes and provide role models.

FINANCIAL INCLUSION: Support initiatives that provide access to financial services for marginalized communities, reducing disparities.

ALLYSHIP: Stand up against financial discrimination and be an ally to those facing stereotypes or biases.

POLICY CHANGES: Advocate for policies that address systemic inequalities and promote economic equity.

By actively addressing financial stereotypes, society can work towards a more inclusive and equitable financial landscape.

DISPELLING MYTHS

THE MYTH OF FINANCIAL DEPENDENCE:

The Myth of Financial Dependence: Challenging Traditional Assumptions

Traditional norms have often perpetuated the idea that financial dependence is undesirable, particularly for adults. This perspective assumes that self-sufficiency in managing one's finances is the only path to personal and financial success. However, it's essential to challenge this myth and recognize the complexities of financial dependence:

INTERDEPENDENCE: In reality, financial interdependence is common and often necessary in various relationships, such as between spouses, family members, or business partners.

SHARED RESPONSIBILITIES: In many households, individuals share financial responsibilities based on their strengths and circumstances. This collaboration doesn't necessarily equate to dependence.

CAREGIVER ROLES: People who take on caregiver roles, whether for children or elderly family members, may temporarily rely on others for support. This doesn't diminish their value or abilities.

ECONOMIC REALITIES: Economic conditions and income disparities can limit someone's ability to achieve full financial independence, making dependence on social safety nets or community support vital.

EMOTIONAL WELL-BEING: Acknowledging and accepting support from others can enhance emotional well-being and strengthen social bonds.

CUSTOMIZATION: Personal finance is not one-size-fits-all. Individuals should be free to define their financial roles and relationships based on what works best for them.
Ultimately, it's important to shift the conversation from stigmatizing financial dependence to fostering healthy financial relationships and promoting individual financial well-being, whatever that may look like.

ADDRESSING STEREOTYPES THAT SUGGEST WOMEN ARE FINANCIALLY DEPENDENT ON OTHERS.

Stereotypes suggesting that women are financially dependent on others are harmful and outdated. To challenge and dismantle these stereotypes, consider the following steps:

1)PROMOTE FINANCIAL LITERACY: Encourage financial education for women to empower them with the knowledge and skills to manage their finances independently.

2) EQUAL OPPORTUNITY: Advocate for equal pay and career opportunities to ensure women have the same financial potential as men.

3) SUPPORTIVE NETWORKS: Create supportive networks and communities where women can share financial advice and experiences, fostering financial independence.

4) ENCOURAGE FINANCIAL GOALS: Encourage women to set and work towards their financial goals, whether that's saving, investing, or starting a business.

5) CHALLENGE BIASES: Actively challenge and confront gender biases when they occur, both in personal and professional settings.

6) FINANCIAL INCLUSION: Promote financial inclusion and accessibility for women, especially in underserved communities.

7) POSITIVE ROLE MODELS: Celebrate and highlight women who have achieved financial independence and success to serve as role models.

8) CULTURAL CHANGE: Work towards broader cultural change by educating and raising awareness

about the importance of gender equality in financial matters.

By addressing these stereotypes and fostering a culture of financial empowerment, we can help women achieve financial independence and break free from outdated notions of dependence.

FINANCIAL CONFIDENCE: Building confidence in managing your finances regardless of your background or previous experiences.

Building financial confidence is essential for anyone, regardless of their background or past experiences. Here's how to nurture financial self-assurance:

1)EDUCATION: Start with financial literacy. Educate yourself about budgeting, saving, investing, and debt management. There are plenty of free online resources and courses available.

2) GOAL SETTING: Define clear financial goals. Having objectives helps you stay motivated and focused on your financial journey.

3) BUDGETING: Create a budget to track income and expenses. This simple tool provides a clear picture of your financial situation and helps you make informed decisions.

4) SMALL STEPS: Begin with small, manageable financial tasks. Gradually tackle more complex financial matters as your confidence grows.

5) SEEK GUIDANCE: Don't hesitate to seek advice from financial professionals or mentors. They can provide valuable insights and guidance.

6) MISTAKES AS LEARNING OPPORTUNITIES: Embrace your financial mistakes as opportunities to learn and improve. Everyone makes them, but they can be valuable lessons.

7) AUTOMATION: Automate savings and bill payments to reduce the mental burden of managing finances and ensure consistency.

8) MONITOR PROGRESS: Regularly review your financial goals and progress. Celebrate your achievements, no matter how small.

9) SELF-COMPASSION: Be patient and kind to yourself. Building financial confidence takes time, and setbacks are a natural part of the process.

10) MINDSET SHIFT: Cultivate a positive and proactive mindset about your financial future. Believing in your ability to improve your financial situation is a crucial step.

Remember that financial confidence is a journey, not a destination. By taking these steps, you can gradually enhance your financial knowledge and skills, empowering yourself to manage your finances effectively, regardless of your background or past experiences.

BREAKING THE GLASS CEILING: How women are shattering traditional gender roles and making strides in high-paying careers.

Women are shattering traditional gender roles and achieving remarkable success in high-paying careers. Several key factors have contributed to this progress:

1)EDUCATION AND SKILLS: Women have gained access to quality education and developed the skills needed for high-paying industries, challenging gender-based stereotypes.

2) ADVOCACY AND SUPPORT: A growing movement for gender equality has led to advocacy for women's rights in the workplace, encouraging more equitable opportunities.

3) MENTORSHIP AND NETWORKING: Women are benefiting from mentorship programs and networking opportunities, helping them navigate and excel in their careers.

4) WORK-LIFE BALANCE: Flexible work arrangements and changing attitudes towards work-life balance have enabled women to pursue demanding careers while balancing personal responsibilities.

5) LEADERSHIP AND REPRESENTATION: Increasing numbers of women are occupying leadership positions, serving as role models and advocates for those following in their footsteps.

6) LEGAL AND POLICY CHANGES: Legislation promoting equal pay and anti-discrimination measures is contributing to a fairer working environment.

As a result, women are increasingly breaking through the glass ceiling, demonstrating their capabilities in fields that were once male-dominated and reshaping the landscape of high-paying careers.

FINANCIAL EDUCATION AND EMPOWERMENT: Key to Financial Well-Being

Financial education and empowerment are essential for individuals to make informed decisions and secure their financial future. Here's why they matter:

Informed Decision-Making: Financial education equips people with the knowledge and skills to make wise financial choices, from budgeting to investing.

Improved Financial Literacy: It fosters a better understanding of financial concepts, reducing vulnerability to scams and poor financial products.

Debt Management: Empowerment helps individuals manage and reduce debt effectively, preventing financial stress.

Savings and Investing: Financial education encourages saving for emergencies and long-term goals, as well as understanding investment options.

Retirement Planning: It ensures individuals plan for their retirement, securing their financial well-being in later years.

Confidence and Control: Financial empowerment instills confidence and a sense of control over one's financial life.

Economic Security: It reduces the risk of financial instability and enhances overall economic security.

Promoting financial education and empowerment is critical to improving the financial well-being of individuals and communities, fostering economic stability and prosperity.

THE IMPORTANCE OF FINANCIAL LITERACY: Empowering women through financial education and knowledge.

Financial literacy is a powerful tool for empowering women and promoting gender equality. Here's why it matters:

Independence: Financial education equips women with the skills to manage their finances independently, reducing dependency on others.

Decision-Making: Knowledge of budgeting, investing, and debt management enables women to make informed financial decisions, enhancing their well-being.

Equal Opportunities: Financial literacy helps women access the same economic opportunities as men, narrowing gender-based financial disparities.

Confidence: With financial knowledge, women gain the confidence to pursue higher-paying careers, entrepreneurship, and investment opportunities.

Economic Security: Understanding savings and investments contributes to women's long-term economic security and retirement planning.

Family Well-Being: Financially literate women can provide better financial guidance to their families, improving their overall quality of life.

By promoting financial literacy, we empower women to take control of their financial futures, participate fully in the economy, and break free from traditional gender-based financial limitations.

TAKING CONTROL: Strategies to take control of your financial destiny and not rely solely on others.

Taking charge of your financial destiny is a critical step toward achieving financial independence. Here are strategies to help you gain control of your finances and reduce reliance on others:

Financial Education: Invest in learning about personal finance. Understand budgeting, investing, debt management, and savings to make informed decisions.

Set Clear Goals: Define specific financial goals, whether it's saving for a home, retirement, or starting a business. Having clear objectives motivates action.

Budgeting: Create a budget to track income and expenses. This helps you manage your money effectively and identify areas where you can save.

Build an Emergency Fund: Save at least three to six months' worth of living expenses in an easily accessible account to handle unexpected financial challenges.

Reduce Debt: Develop a plan to pay off high-interest debts, such as credit card balances, as quickly as possible to regain financial control.

Invest Wisely: Start investing to grow your wealth over time. Consider a diversified portfolio of stocks, bonds, or real estate, based on your risk tolerance and goals.

Increase Income: Explore opportunities for career advancement, side hustles, or entrepreneurship to boost your earning potential.

Protect Your Finances: Obtain insurance coverage to safeguard against unexpected events like illness, accidents, or property damage.

Continual Learning: Stay updated on financial trends and strategies to adapt and optimize your financial plan.

Seek Professional Guidance: Consult financial advisors or experts when needed to make the most of your financial situation.

Remember, taking control of your financial destiny is a journey that requires dedication and discipline. With these strategies, you can shape your financial future and reduce reliance on others for financial stability.

SEEKING SUPPORT: The role of mentors, advisors, and financial professionals in your journey to financial empowerment.

Mentors, advisors, and financial professionals play vital roles in your path to financial empowerment:

Mentors: Experienced individuals can provide guidance, share insights, and offer support based on their own financial journeys.

Advisors: Certified financial advisors offer personalized financial planning, helping you set and achieve financial goals while navigating complex financial decisions.

Financial Professionals: Experts in areas like investing, tax planning, or estate planning provide specialized knowledge to optimize your financial strategy.

Their expertise and guidance can be invaluable as you work toward financial empowerment, helping you make informed decisions and overcome challenges on your path to financial independence.

THE GENDER WAGE GAP

The Gender Wage Gap: A Persistent Inequality

The gender wage gap is a long-standing issue that reflects disparities in earnings between men and women. Key points about the gender wage gap include:

Earnings Disparity: On average, women tend to earn less than men for similar work. This wage gap exists across various industries and job levels.

Complex Causes: The gender wage gap has multiple causes, including discrimination, occupational segregation (women in lower-paying fields), and differences in work experience.

Motherhood Penalty: Women often experience reduced earning potential after becoming mothers, due to factors like reduced work hours and opportunities.

Intersectionality: The wage gap is more pronounced for women of color, highlighting the intersection of gender and racial inequalities.

Legislative Measures: Various countries have enacted laws and policies to address wage gap issues, such as equal pay legislation and family leave policies.

Social Awareness: Advocacy and awareness campaigns aim to challenge stereotypes, biases, and societal norms that contribute to the wage gap.

Efforts to reduce the gender wage gap focus on promoting pay equity, supporting women's career advancement, and addressing structural inequalities. Achieving wage equality is a crucial step toward gender equality in the workplace.

UNDERSTANDING THE GAP

FACTS AND FIGURES: An overview of the gender wage gap and its impact on women's financial well-being.

In the United States, women typically earn about 82 cents for every dollar earned by men, representing a persistent gender wage gap.

The gap is even wider for women of color. Hispanic and Black women, on average, earn less than white women in comparison to white men.

The wage gap's cumulative effect results in significantly lower lifetime earnings for women, affecting their ability to save, invest, and secure their financial future.
The motherhood penalty compounds the issue, with mothers experiencing a wage gap that often extends throughout their careers.

Lower earnings can lead to reduced retirement savings, impacting women's long-term financial security.
Bridging the gender wage gap is not only a matter of economic justice but also crucial for ensuring women's financial empowerment and equality in society.

CONTRIBUTING FACTORS: Examining the factors that contribute to the wage gap, including occupational segregation and negotiation disparities.

The gender wage gap is influenced by several contributing factors, including:

Occupational Segregation: Women are often concentrated in lower-paying fields, contributing to the overall wage gap. They are underrepresented in high-paying STEM and leadership roles.

Negotiation Disparities: Research shows that women may be less likely to negotiate their salaries or promotions compared to men, which can lead to lower earnings over time.

Stereotypes and Bias: Gender stereotypes and biases can influence hiring and promotion decisions, limiting women's access to high-paying positions.

Motherhood Penalty: Women who become mothers often face reduced earning potential due to factors like reduced work hours and discriminatory practices.

Lack of Equal Opportunities: Unequal access to career advancement opportunities, mentorship, and training can also contribute to the wage gap.

Addressing these factors is crucial for reducing the wage gap and achieving greater gender pay equity, creating a more inclusive and financially equitable workforce.

EQUAL PAY ADVOCACY: The importance of advocating for equal pay and working towards closing the gap.

Advocating for equal pay is essential for several reasons:

Economic Justice: Equal pay is a matter of fairness, ensuring that individuals are compensated based on their skills and contributions rather than their gender.

Women's Empowerment: Closing the wage gap empowers women economically, allowing them to invest, save, and plan for their financial future with the same opportunities as men.

Economic Growth: Reducing the wage gap can stimulate economic growth by increasing women's earning potential and contributing to overall prosperity.

Social Equity: Achieving pay equity is a step toward greater gender equality, promoting a more inclusive and just society.

Global Impact: Equal pay advocacy has international implications, influencing global discussions on gender equity and labor rights.

By advocating for equal pay and supporting policies and practices that promote wage parity, we can work towards a more equitable and economically just future for all individuals, regardless of gender.

FEMALE WEALTH ROLE MODELS

FINDING INSPIRATION:

WOMEN WHO LEAD: Stories of successful women who have achieved financial independence and the paths they took.

Many successful women have broken barriers, achieved financial independence, and become trailblazers in their respective fields. Their stories offer valuable lessons and inspiration:

1)OPRAH WINFREY: From a troubled childhood, Oprah rose to become a media mogul. Her influential talk show, investments, and philanthropy have earned her financial independence and a net worth in the billions.

2) SHERYL SANDBERG: Facebook's COO, Sheryl Sandberg, exemplifies success in the tech industry. She's known for her leadership, advocacy for women in tech, and bestselling book "Lean In."

3) INDRA NOOYI: As the former CEO of PepsiCo, Indra Nooyi steered the company to remarkable success. Her leadership and commitment to diversity made her a standout figure in corporate America.

4) RUTH BADER GINSBURG: The late Supreme Court Justice Ginsburg was a symbol of gender equality. Her legal career and advocacy for women's rights made her an iconic figure.

5) MARY BARRR: As the CEO of General Motors, Mary Barra broke through the automotive industry's glass ceiling. Her dedication to innovation and sustainability has solidified her position.

6) ARIANNA HUFFINGTON: The co-founder of The Huffington Post, Arianna Huffington, created a media empire. Her journey emphasizes resilience and reinvention.

7) SARA BLAKELY: The founder of Spanx, Sara Blakely turned an innovative idea into a billion-dollar business. Her entrepreneurial spirit and determination are inspiring.

8) GWYNNE SHOTWELL: As the President and COO of SpaceX, Gwynne Shotwell has played a pivotal role in advancing space exploration. Her leadership in a male-dominated industry is noteworthy.

9) MELLODY HOBSON: The co-CEO and President of Ariel Investments, Mellody Hobson is a prominent figure in finance. She's known for her financial expertise and advocacy for diversity.

10) MALALA YOUSAFZAI: The youngest Nobel laureate, Malala Yousafzai, advocates for girls' education worldwide. Her journey from surviving an attack to becoming a global symbol of education is remarkable.

These women's journeys to financial independence are characterized by hard work, resilience, and a commitment to their goals. Their stories serve as a testament to the possibilities that exist for women in various fields and inspire others to pursue their own paths to financial success.

MENTORSHIP AND NETWORKING: The value of connecting with other successful women and learning from their experiences.

Connecting with successful women through mentorship and networking can be invaluable:

Guidance: Mentors offer guidance, sharing their experiences, insights, and advice to help navigate challenges and make informed decisions.

Inspiration: Learning from the achievements of other successful women can be deeply inspiring, motivating individuals to pursue their own goals.

Expanded Opportunities: Networking opens doors to new opportunities, collaborations, and partnerships, enhancing career and business prospects.

Empowerment: Building a support network of like-minded women can provide emotional and professional support, empowering individuals to overcome obstacles.

By seeking mentorship and expanding your network, you can tap into the collective wisdom and experiences of successful women, accelerating your path to financial independence and personal growth.

THE POWER OF REPRESENTATION: How seeing women in influential financial roles can inspire the next generation.

Seeing women in influential financial roles can have a profound impact:

Inspiration: Female role models in finance demonstrate what's possible, inspiring young women to pursue careers in this field.

Breaking Stereotypes: Representation challenges gender stereotypes and empowers individuals to follow their passions, regardless of traditional expectations.

Pathways to Success: Learning about the journeys of successful women in finance provides guidance and insights for the next generation.

Diversity of Thought: Greater gender diversity in financial leadership fosters a diversity of thought, leading to more innovative and inclusive financial strategies.

By showcasing women in influential financial roles, we encourage a more diverse and equitable financial landscape and empower future generations to aim high in their financial pursuits.

Having a deeper understanding of the financial dynamics women face in today's world is vital. You need to be equipped with strategies to overcome financial stereotypes, advocate for equal pay, and seek inspiration from female role models who have achieved financial success. This chapter is a pivotal resource for women looking to navigate and thrive in the ever-evolving landscape of personal finance, helping you take charge of your financial future with confidence and determination.

CHAPTER SEVEN

PROTECTING YOUR WEALTH

INTRODUCTION

We will delve into the crucial aspect of safeguarding your financial well-being. Protecting your wealth is just as important as building it. This chapter explores insurance essentials, estate planning, and strategies for avoiding common financial pitfalls.

INSURANCE ESSENTIALS

THE ROLE OF INSURANCE

FINANCIAL SECURITY: How insurance provides a safety net for unexpected events:

Financial security is a critical aspect of one's overall well-being, and insurance plays a pivotal role in providing a safety net for unexpected events. Insurance is a financial product that helps individuals, businesses, and even governments mitigate the financial risks associated with various unforeseen circumstances. These circumstances can include accidents, illnesses, natural disasters, and more. Let's explore how insurance contributes to financial security:

RISK TRANSFER: Insurance enables individuals and organizations to transfer the financial risk of potential losses to an insurance company. In exchange for regular premium payments, the insurer promises to provide compensation in the event of a covered loss. This transfer of risk helps protect policyholders from experiencing significant financial hardships due to unexpected events.

PROTECTION AGAINST PROPERTY LOSS: Property insurance, including homeowner's insurance and renters' insurance, safeguards against the financial impact of damage or loss to one's property. In the case of natural disasters, theft, or accidents, insurance can cover the repair or replacement costs, preventing a substantial financial burden.

HEALTHCARE COVERAGE: Health insurance is an integral part of financial security. It ensures access to medical care without incurring exorbitant expenses. In countries with universal healthcare, insurance may still be necessary for supplementary coverage or specialized treatments.

LIFE INSURANCE: Life insurance provides financial protection to the beneficiaries of the insured individual in case of their death. This protection ensures that dependents are financially secure, covering funeral expenses, debt repayment, and ongoing living costs.

INCOME PROTECTION: Disability insurance and long-term care insurance offer income protection if an individual becomes unable to work due to illness or injury. These policies provide regular income to help meet daily expenses and healthcare needs.

LIABILITY COVERAGE: Liability insurance, whether in the context of auto insurance, homeowners' insurance, or business insurance, safeguards policyholders from legal and financial liabilities in the event they are responsible for causing harm to others or damaging their property.

BUSINESS CONTINUITY: Business insurance, including property, liability, and business interruption insurance, is vital for entrepreneurs and organizations. It ensures that a sudden event, such as a fire or a lawsuit, does not lead to financial ruin or bankruptcy.

RISK DIVERSIFICATION: Insurance operates on the principle of risk pooling and diversification. Policyholders collectively contribute premiums, which are then used to compensate those who experience losses. This spreads the financial risk across a broad group of people, making it more manageable for each individual.

PEACE OF MIND: Beyond financial protection, insurance offers peace of mind. Knowing that you have a safety net in place can reduce stress and anxiety associated with potential financial setbacks, allowing individuals and families to focus on other aspects of their lives.

LEGAL AND CONTRACTUAL OBLIGATIONS: In many cases, insurance is a legal or contractual requirement. For example, auto insurance is mandatory in most countries to cover potential damages in accidents. Lenders may also require insurance on financed assets like homes or vehicles.

In summary, insurance is a crucial component of financial security, offering protection against various unexpected events that could otherwise result in substantial financial distress. It acts as a safety net, allowing individuals and entities to mitigate risk, protect their assets, and ensure their financial well-being. Careful consideration of one's insurance needs and prudent selection of policies are key steps in achieving comprehensive financial security.

TYPES OF INSURANCE: AN OVERVIEW OF VARIOUS INSURANCE TYPES,INCLUDING HEALTH,AUTO,HOME,LIFE, AND DISABILITY INSURANCE.

Insurance is a diverse industry that offers a wide range of coverage options tailored to meet the specific needs of individuals, businesses, and organizations.

HEALTH INSURANCE: This type of insurance covers medical expenses, including doctor visits, hospital stays, and prescription medications. Health insurance can be provided by employers, government programs (e.g., Medicare and Medicaid in the U.S.), or purchased individually. It plays a vital role in ensuring access to healthcare services and protecting individuals from high medical bills.

AUTO INSURANCE: Auto insurance is mandatory in most places and covers costs related to accidents and vehicle damage. It includes liability coverage, collision coverage for your vehicle, and comprehensive coverage for non-collision events like theft.

HOME INSURANCE: Home insurance, which includes homeowners and renters' insurance, protects against property damage and personal belongings loss. It covers structural damage, personal property, liability, and additional living expenses in case your home becomes uninhabitable.

LIFE INSURANCE: Life insurance provides a payout to beneficiaries upon the death of the insured person. It can be term life insurance (for a specific term) or permanent life insurance (lifelong coverage), serving as a financial safety net for dependents.

DISABILITY INSURANCE: Disability insurance offers income replacement if you become disabled and cannot work. There are short-term and long-term disability options, ensuring you can meet daily expenses and healthcare needs.

BUSINESS INSURANCE: Business Insurance includes various types like property insurance, liability insurance, workers' compensation, and more.
Property insurance covers business assets and premises. Liability insurance protects against legal claims. Workers' compensation provides coverage for employee injuries.
Business insurance is crucial for safeguarding an organization's financial stability and protecting against unforeseen risks.

PET INSURANCE:
Pet Insurance helps cover veterinary expenses for pets, including accidents, illnesses, and routine care.
It ensures that pet owners can provide proper medical care for their animals without being burdened by high vet bills.

SPECIALTY INSURANCE:
Various specialty insurance types cater to unique needs, including flood insurance, earthquake insurance, professional liability insurance, and more.

These types of insurance play vital roles in protecting individuals, families, and assets from various risks and unexpected events, ensuring financial security in different aspects of life.

These policies offer specialized protection for specific risks that may not be adequately covered by standard insurance plans.
In conclusion, insurance is a crucial tool for managing risk and ensuring financial security in various aspects of life, from healthcare and auto ownership to homeownership, income protection, and even travel. Understanding the different types of insurance and selecting policies that align with individual or business needs is essential to mitigate financial vulnerabilities and unexpected challenges.

ASSESSING NEEDS: Determine the appropriate level of insurance coverage for your unique circumstances.

Health Insurance

Assessing your needs for health insurance involves considering several factors to determine the appropriate level of coverage for your unique circumstances:

HEALTHCARE NEEDS: Evaluate your medical history, current health status, and any ongoing conditions or prescriptions. Consider how often you require medical care, such as doctor visits, specialist consultations, or medications.

FAMILY SITUATION: If you have dependents, assess their healthcare needs as well. You may need coverage for family members, including children or a spouse.

BUDGET: Consider your budget and how much you can comfortably allocate to health insurance premiums. Weigh this against potential out-of-pocket costs like deductibles and copayments.

RISK TOLERANCE: Assess your risk tolerance. Are you comfortable with higher deductibles and lower premiums, or do you prefer more comprehensive coverage with higher upfront costs?

NETWORK: Ensure that your preferred healthcare providers, including doctors and hospitals, are within the insurance network to minimize out-of-pocket expenses.

LEGAL REQUIREMENTS: Be aware of any legal requirements regarding health insurance, such as the mandate to have coverage in some countries.

LIFE CHANGES: Anticipate potential life changes, like a new job, retirement, or additions to your family, as they can impact your healthcare needs.

By carefully considering these factors, you can tailor your health insurance coverage to align with your specific needs and financial situation. It's often a balance between ensuring adequate coverage while managing costs effectively.

UNDERSTANDING COVERAGE: Navigating health insurance plans, including deductibles, premiums, and copayments.Understanding coverage in health insurance involves grasping key components like deductibles, which are initial out-of-pocket costs, premiums, regular payments to maintain the policy, and copayments, fixed fees for medical services. Choosing the right balance between these factors is crucial for tailored coverage that suits your healthcare needs and budget.

LONG-TERM CARE: Long-term care insurance helps you plan for future healthcare needs that may arise due to aging, disability, or chronic illness. It covers services like nursing home care, assisted living, and in-home assistance. Investing in such insurance can provide financial security, ensuring you receive the necessary care without depleting your savings or burdening your family. It's a proactive step in safeguarding your well-being and peace of mind as you age.

PROPERTY AND ASSET

Home Insurance: Protecting your property through homeowners or renters insurance.

Auto Insurance: Ensuring your vehicles are adequately covered.

Valuables and Personal Property: Strategies for safeguarding valuable possessions.
Estate Planning

WILLS AND TRUSTS

THE IMPORTANCE OF ESTATE PLANNING: Estate planning is vital for ensuring that your assets are distributed in accordance with your wishes after you pass away. It involves creating a comprehensive plan that can minimize estate taxes, avoid legal disputes, and provide for your loved ones. By clearly outlining your intentions through wills, trusts, and other legal documents, you maintain control over how your legacy is managed, helping to protect your family's financial future and your personal values even when you're no longer here.

WILLS vs. TRUSTS

Wills and trusts serve distinct purposes in estate planning:

WILLS:
A will is a legal document that outlines your wishes for the distribution of assets after your death.
It can name guardians for minor children and an executor to carry out your wishes.
Wills go through probate, a legal process that can be time-consuming and costly.

TRUSTS:
A trust is a legal arrangement that holds and manages assets for the benefit of specific individuals or entities.
It can avoid probate, allowing for a faster and private asset transfer.
Trusts are often used for more complex situations, like managing assets for minors, protecting assets from creditors, or ensuring ongoing care for someone with special needs.

WHEN TO USE EACH:

Wills are typically suitable for simpler estates or when you have few assets and straightforward wishes.

Trusts are preferred when you seek more control over how and when assets are distributed, want to avoid probate, or have complex financial situations.

A combination of both may also be appropriate for comprehensive estate planning, tailored to your unique circumstances. It's advisable to consult with an attorney to determine the best approach for your needs.

NAMING BENEFICIARIES:

Naming beneficiaries is a crucial aspect of financial and estate planning to ensure that your assets go to the intended individuals or entities. Here's why it's important:

CLARITY OF INTENT: Designating beneficiaries in various financial accounts, life insurance policies, retirement plans, and in your will clarifies your wishes, leaving no room for ambiguity.

AVOIDING PROBATE: Assets with designated beneficiaries can often bypass probate, streamlining the transfer process and saving time and money.

IMMEDIATE TRANSFER: Upon your passing, assets with named beneficiaries typically transfer quickly to the recipients, providing much-needed financial support.

CONTROL: You maintain control over who receives your assets, allowing you to provide for loved ones, charities, or organizations that matter to you.

PROTECTION: Beneficiary designations can help protect assets from creditors or legal disputes, ensuring they benefit your chosen recipients.

It's essential to periodically review and update your beneficiary designations, especially after major life events like marriage, divorce, or the birth of children. Ensure your selections align with your current wishes and circumstances to guarantee your assets go to the right people or entities when the time comes.

POWERS OF ATTORNEY AND HEALTHCARE DIRECTIVES

LEGAL DECISION-MAKING: Appointing trusted individuals to make financial and healthcare decisions on your behalf if you're unable to do so.

END-OF-LIFE CARE: Documenting your wishes for end-of-life medical care through advance healthcare directives.

AVOIDING FINANCIAL PITFALLS

COMMON FINANCIAL MISTAKES

SPENDING BEYOND MEANS: Strategies for living within your financial means.

Spending beyond your means can lead to financial stress and debt. To live within your financial means, consider these strategies:

1)BUDGETING: Create a realistic budget to track income and expenses. This helps identify areas where you can cut back.

2) EMERGENCY FUND: Build an emergency fund to cover unexpected expenses, reducing the need for credit or loans.

3) PRIORITIZE NEEDS OVER WANTS: Distinguish between essential expenses (needs) and discretionary spending (wants). Focus on needs first.

4) DEBT MANAGEMENT: If you have debt, prioritize paying it down. High-interest debts, like credit cards, should be tackled first.

5)SAVINGS GOALS: Set specific savings goals, whether for retirement, education, or a major purchase. Automate contributions to savings accounts.

6) LIVE BELOW YOUR MEANS: Aim to spend less than you earn. This creates a financial cushion and reduces stress.

7) CUT UNNECESSARY EXPENSES: Review your spending habits and identify areas where you can cut back, such as dining out less or canceling unused subscriptions.

8) INCREASE INCOME: Consider ways to boost your income, such as a side job, freelancing, or investing in education for better job opportunities.

9) FINANCIAL EDUCATION: Continuously educate yourself about personal finance. Understanding money management is key to living within your means.

10) DELAYED GRATIFICATION: Practice delayed gratification by saving for purchases rather than relying on credit.

11) SEEK PROFESSIONAL ADVICE: If you're struggling with finances, consult a financial advisor or counselor for guidance.

Remember that living within your means is essential for long-term financial stability. It may require discipline and adjustments, but the peace of mind and reduced financial stress are well worth the effort.

FAILURE TO SAVE: Failure to save can have significant consequences for your financial well-being. Here's why consistent saving is crucial:

Financial Security: Saving provides a safety net for unexpected expenses, ensuring you're not caught off guard by emergencies.

Long-Term Goals: Regular savings help you work toward long-term goals like homeownership, retirement, or education without relying on loans or credit.

Compound Growth: Saving and investing early allows your money to grow through compound interest, potentially multiplying your wealth over time.

Retirement Planning: Saving for retirement is essential to maintain your quality of life once you stop working. Neglecting this can lead to financial difficulties in your later years.

Reduced Stress: Knowing you have savings eases financial stress, allowing you to handle life's ups and downs more effectively.

Freedom and Opportunities: Savings can provide the freedom to explore new opportunities, change careers, or start a business.

Legacy Planning: Saving enables you to leave a financial legacy for your loved ones or support charitable causes.

To make saving a habit, consider automating transfers to a savings account, setting specific savings goals, and living within your means. Start small if necessary, but start today, as consistent saving is a key to financial stability and future success.

IGNORING DEBT:

Ignoring debt can lead to financial trouble, but effective debt management can help regain control. Here are strategies to tackle debt:

Assessment: Start by listing all your debts, including balances, interest rates, and minimum payments.

Budgeting: Create a budget to allocate a portion of your income toward debt repayment.

Priority Payments: Focus on high-interest debt first, as paying it off saves money in the long run.

Consolidation: Consider debt consolidation to combine multiple debts into one with a lower interest rate.

Snowball or Avalanche Method: Choose a debt repayment strategy that suits you. The snowball method prioritizes paying off the smallest debts first, while the avalanche method focuses on the highest interest debts.

Cut Expenses: Reduce discretionary spending to free up more money for debt payments.

Extra Income: Look for additional sources of income, like a part-time job or selling unused items.

Negotiate Interest Rates: Contact creditors to negotiate lower interest rates or explore debt management programs.

Emergency Fund: Maintain an emergency fund to avoid relying on credit in case of unexpected expenses.

Credit Counseling: Seek guidance from a credit counselor to develop a debt management plan.

Avoid Accumulating More Debt: Stop using credit cards or taking on new debt while repaying existing obligations.

Stay Committed: Debt reduction may take time. Stay committed to your plan and track your progress.

Managing and reducing debt is a proactive step toward financial freedom and stability. It requires discipline and patience, but with the right approach, you can regain control of your finances and work towards a debt-free future.

SCAMS AND FRAUD PREVENTION

RECOGNIZING SCAMS:

Recognizing financial scams is crucial to protect yourself from fraud. Here are common scams and tips to identify them:

Phishing Emails: Scammers send fake emails posing as legitimate institutions, often with suspicious links or requests for personal information. Look for misspellings, generic greetings, and verify the sender's email address.

Phone Scams: Fraudsters may impersonate government agencies, banks, or tech support. They pressure you for immediate action or payment. Be cautious of unsolicited calls and verify their identity independently.

Social Engineering: Scammers use personal information to manipulate you. Beware of unsolicited requests for personal or financial details.

Online Shopping Scams: Avoid deals that seem too good to be true, especially on unfamiliar websites. Look for secure payment methods and read reviews.

Investment Scams: Be cautious of guaranteed high returns, unsolicited investment offers, or unregistered investments. Research and verify investment opportunities.

Romance Scams: Online scammers build emotional connections to solicit money. Beware of requests for financial help from people you've never met in person.

Sweepstakes and Lottery Scams: You're told you've won a prize but need to pay fees or taxes to claim it. Legitimate lotteries don't ask for upfront payments.

Identity Theft: Monitor your accounts for unusual activity and protect your personal information. Consider identity theft protection services.

Tech Support Scams: Unsolicited calls claim your computer is infected. Legitimate tech support won't cold call you.

Charity Scams: Verify charities before donating, especially after natural disasters. Scammers exploit people's goodwill.

Ponzi Schemes: Beware of investment opportunities that rely on new investors' money to pay previous investors. Ensure the investment is legitimate and registered.

Government Impersonation: Scammers may pretend to be from the IRS or other government agencies. Verify their identity independently.

Stay informed, trust your instincts, and don't rush into financial decisions. If something seems suspicious, research and seek advice from trusted sources. Protecting your financial well-being requires vigilance and skepticism when dealing with unfamiliar or unsolicited financial offers.

If you take your time to read through this chapter, you'll have a comprehensive understanding of how to protect your wealth and ensure your financial security. You'll know the importance of insurance in mitigating risks, the significance of estate planning for asset distribution, and how to avoid common financial pitfalls. Armed with this knowledge, you'll be well-prepared to safeguard your financial well-being and make informed decisions to protect your wealth for yourself and future generations.

CHAPTER EIGHT

BUILDING A SUPPORTIVE FINANCIAL COMMUNITY

INTRODUCTION

In this chapter, we explore the importance of building a supportive financial community. Your journey to financial empowerment is not one you have to take alone. This chapter delves into networking for success, the power of mentorship and collaboration, and the importance of passing on financial literacy to future generations.

NETWORKING FOR SUCCESS

BUILDING YOUR NETWORK

THE POWER OF CONNECTIONS:

The power of connections and networking is undeniable in creating opportunities and advancing your personal and professional life. Here's why it matters:

Access to Resources: Networking broadens your access to resources, information, and knowledge that you might not discover on your own.

Job Opportunities: Many job openings are never advertised. Networking can connect you with professionals who know of unadvertised positions.

Learning and Growth: Interacting with diverse individuals exposes you to new perspectives, insights, and skill sets, promoting personal and professional growth.

Collaboration and Partnerships: Networking can lead to collaborations, partnerships, and business opportunities, enhancing your reach and impact.

Mentorship: You can find mentors or role models who provide guidance, support, and valuable advice on your journey.

Confidence Building: Networking hones your interpersonal skills, boosting your confidence in social and professional settings.

Reputation Building: Building strong connections can enhance your reputation and credibility in your field or industry.

Information Exchange: Networking provides a platform for the exchange of industry trends, best practices, and market insights.

Support System: A robust network can offer emotional support during challenging times and celebrate your successes with you.

Serendipity: Chance encounters and conversations often lead to unexpected opportunities and breakthroughs.

To make the most of networking, be genuine, generous, and proactive. Attend industry events, join professional organizations, and engage on social media platforms. Building meaningful connections takes time, but the dividends it pays in terms of opportunities, personal growth, and a supportive community are well worth the effort.

NETWORKING STRATEGIES: Tips for expanding your professional and financial network.

Expanding your professional and financial network is essential for personal and career growth. Here are some effective networking strategies:

1)Set Clear Goals: Define your objectives for networking, whether it's finding a job, growing your business, or gaining industry insights.

2) Attend Events: Attend conferences, seminars, workshops, and industry-specific events. These are great places to meet like-minded individuals.

3) Utilize Social Media: Engage on platforms like LinkedIn, Twitter, and industry forums. Share your expertise and connect with professionals.

4) Volunteer: Offer your skills or time to non-profit organizations, events, or causes. It's an excellent way to meet people with similar values.

5) Join Professional Organizations: Become a member of associations related to your field. They often host networking events and provide resources.

6) Leverage Alumni Networks: Connect with former classmates and colleagues. Your alma mater can be a valuable networking resource.

7) Be a Good Listener: Pay attention to others during conversations, ask questions, and show genuine interest in their stories.

8) Follow Up: After meeting someone, send a personalized follow-up message. Maintain the connection with occasional updates or shared resources.

9) Provide Value: Offer assistance, insights, or resources to your connections. Being a resourceful contact can strengthen relationships.

10) Diversify Contacts: Aim to build a diverse network including people from various industries, backgrounds, and experience levels.

11) Develop Elevator Pitch: Prepare a concise introduction that highlights your skills and goals. It's handy for making a strong first impression.

12) Build Online Presence: Create and maintain a professional online presence through a well-crafted LinkedIn profile or personal website.

13) Mentorship and Coaching: Seek mentors and offer mentorship to others. These relationships can be mutually beneficial.

14) Local Networking: Attend local events and join community organizations to expand your network in your area.

15) Stay Informed: Keep up with industry news and trends to have informed conversations with your network.

Remember that effective networking is not just about what you can gain but also what you can offer. It's a two-way street that involves building mutually beneficial relationships over time.

ONLINE vs. IN-PERSON NETWORKING: Leveraging both digital and real-world networking opportunities.

Online and in-person networking each offer distinct advantages, and a well-rounded strategy leverages both:

ONLINE NETWORKING:

1)Global Reach: Online platforms, like LinkedIn and professional forums, allow you to connect with individuals worldwide.

2) Convenience: You can network from anywhere, at any time, making it highly flexible.

3) Efficiency: Quick exchanges of information and resources are possible, ideal for busy professionals.

4) Rich Information: Online profiles offer comprehensive information about potential contacts, helping you identify common interests and goals.

5) Diverse Platforms: A variety of platforms cater to different networking goals, from career advancement to entrepreneurial opportunities.

IN-PERSON NETWORKING :

1)Personal Connection: Face-to-face meetings allow for deeper, more personal connections and can build trust more effectively.

2) Non-Verbal Communication: In-person interactions provide cues beyond words, such as body language and tone of voice.

3) Serendipity: Chance meetings at conferences or events can lead to unexpected opportunities and collaborations.

4) Networking Events: Specific gatherings are dedicated to networking, creating a focused environment for making connections.

5) Local Relevance: In-person networking can be particularly effective for building relationships within a local community or industry.

LEVERAGING BOTH:

1)Hybrid Approach: Use online platforms to identify potential contacts and schedule in-person meetings for stronger connections.

2) Follow-Up: After an in-person meeting, connect with new contacts on social media to stay in

touch and share updates.

3) Virtual Events: Attend online versions of conferences or industry events when attending in person is not feasible.

4) Reciprocity: Offer to meet connections from online platforms in person when geography allows, reinforcing the relationship.

5) Adapt to Circumstances: Balance your approach based on your goals, the nature of your industry, and current circumstances (e.g., remote work or travel restrictions).

Both online and in-person networking are valuable, and the right mix depends on your specific objectives and preferences. A diversified strategy allows you to harness the strengths of each approach for a more comprehensive networking experience.

PERSONAL BRANDING

CRAFTING YOUR IMAGE: Strategies for building a personal brand that aligns with your financial goals.

Building a personal brand that aligns with your financial goals is essential for career success and financial well-being. Here are strategies to craft your image effectively:

1)Self-Reflection: Understand your values, strengths, and long-term financial objectives. Your personal brand should reflect these elements.

2) Consistency: Maintain a consistent image across various platforms, including social media, your resume, and personal interactions.

3) Professional Appearance: Dress and present yourself in a way that aligns with your industry and financial goals.

4) Online Presence: Curate your online presence, especially on professional networks like LinkedIn. Share content related to your field and achievements.

5) Authenticity: Be true to yourself. Authenticity is a key element of a strong personal brand.

6) Professional Development: Invest in skills and education to continuously improve your value and marketability.

7) Networking: Cultivate a network of contacts in your industry who can endorse and recommend you.

8) Value Proposition: Define what sets you apart from others in your field. Highlight your unique skills and achievements.

9) Public Speaking and Writing: Opportunities to speak or write in your area of expertise can enhance your reputation.

10) Testimonials and Recommendations: Encourage colleagues, mentors, and clients to provide testimonials that can be displayed on your website or LinkedIn profile.

11) Mentorship: Seek guidance from mentors who have achieved financial success in your field.

12) Public Relations: If appropriate, consider hiring a public relations professional to help shape and maintain your personal brand.

13) Professional Headshot: A high-quality headshot adds a professional touch to your personal brand.

14) Reputation Management: Monitor your online presence and address any negative feedback or misinformation promptly.

15) Elevator Pitch: Develop a concise statement that introduces you and your value within your industry.

Your personal brand is an ongoing project, requiring consistent effort and evolution. Aligning it with your financial goals can enhance your career opportunities, earning potential, and overall financial well-being.

ONLINE PRESENCE: Utilizing social media and online platforms to enhance your personal brand.

Leveraging social media and online platforms is crucial for enhancing your personal brand. Here are a few ways to make the most of your online presence:

1)Choose the Right Platforms: Focus on platforms relevant to your industry and target audience. For professional branding, LinkedIn is essential, while platforms like Twitter, Instagram, or a personal website may also be beneficial.

2) Consistent Branding: Use a consistent profile picture, bio, and messaging across platforms to reinforce your brand identity.

3) Content Sharing: Share valuable, industry-related content, including articles, news, and your insights. Regularly post updates to showcase your expertise.

4) Engagement: Interact with your connections and followers by commenting on their posts,

responding to messages, and participating in relevant discussions.

5) Thought Leadership: Position yourself as a thought leader in your field by creating and sharing your original content, such as blog posts, videos, or podcasts.

6) Networking: Actively connect with professionals, colleagues, and mentors in your industry to expand your network.

7) Recommendations and Endorsements: Seek endorsements and recommendations from colleagues and clients to build credibility.

8) Privacy Settings: Be mindful of privacy settings and what you share publicly. Protect personal information.

9) Manage Your Online Image: Regularly Google your name to see what information appears about you online. Address any discrepancies or negative content.

10) Use Keywords: Incorporate relevant keywords in your profiles and content to improve search engine visibility.

11) Participate in Groups: Join industry-specific groups or forums on platforms like LinkedIn to engage with like-minded professionals.

12) Online Courses and Certifications: Highlight any online courses or certifications you've completed on your profiles.

13) Showcase Achievements: Share your professional accomplishments, awards, and milestones.

14) Engage in Personal Branding Workshops: Consider participating in personal branding workshops or courses to refine your online presence.

15) Monitor Analytics: Track the performance of your online content and adjust your strategy based on what resonates with your audience.

A strong online presence can boost your visibility, reputation, and credibility, ultimately helping you achieve your personal and financial goals. Remember to maintain a professional and positive tone, as your online presence often serves as the first impression potential employers, clients, and partners have of you.

MENTORSHIP AND COLLABORATION

THE VALUE OF MENTORSHIP

MENTORSHIP BENEFITS: Mentorship can accelerate your learning and personal growth.

Mentorship offers several benefits, including:

Accelerated Learning: Mentors provide guidance, knowledge, and experience, helping you learn faster and avoid common pitfalls.

Personal Growth: Mentors offer valuable insights and encouragement, fostering your personal and professional development.

Networking: Mentors can introduce you to valuable contacts, expanding your network and opening up opportunities.

Accountability: A mentor can hold you accountable for your goals and help you stay on track.

Confidence Building: Guidance from a mentor boosts your confidence, enabling you to tackle challenges with more assurance.

Career Advancement: Mentorship often leads to career advancement, as mentors help you navigate your industry and make informed decisions.

FINDING A MENTOR: Strategies for identifying and approaching potential mentors.

To find a mentor, consider these strategies:

Clarify Your Goals: Define what you hope to gain from mentorship, which will help you identify the right mentor.

Leverage Existing Connections: Reach out to colleagues, friends, or alumni networks for potential mentor recommendations.

Online Platforms: Use LinkedIn or professional organizations to identify experienced individuals in your field.

Attend Networking Events: Attend industry-specific conferences, seminars, and workshops to meet potential mentors in person.

Ask for Introductions: Request introductions from mutual contacts who may know potential mentors.

Cold Outreach: Send a polite, well-crafted message explaining your goals and why you'd like to be mentored.

Be Specific: When approaching someone, be clear about your expectations and how their expertise

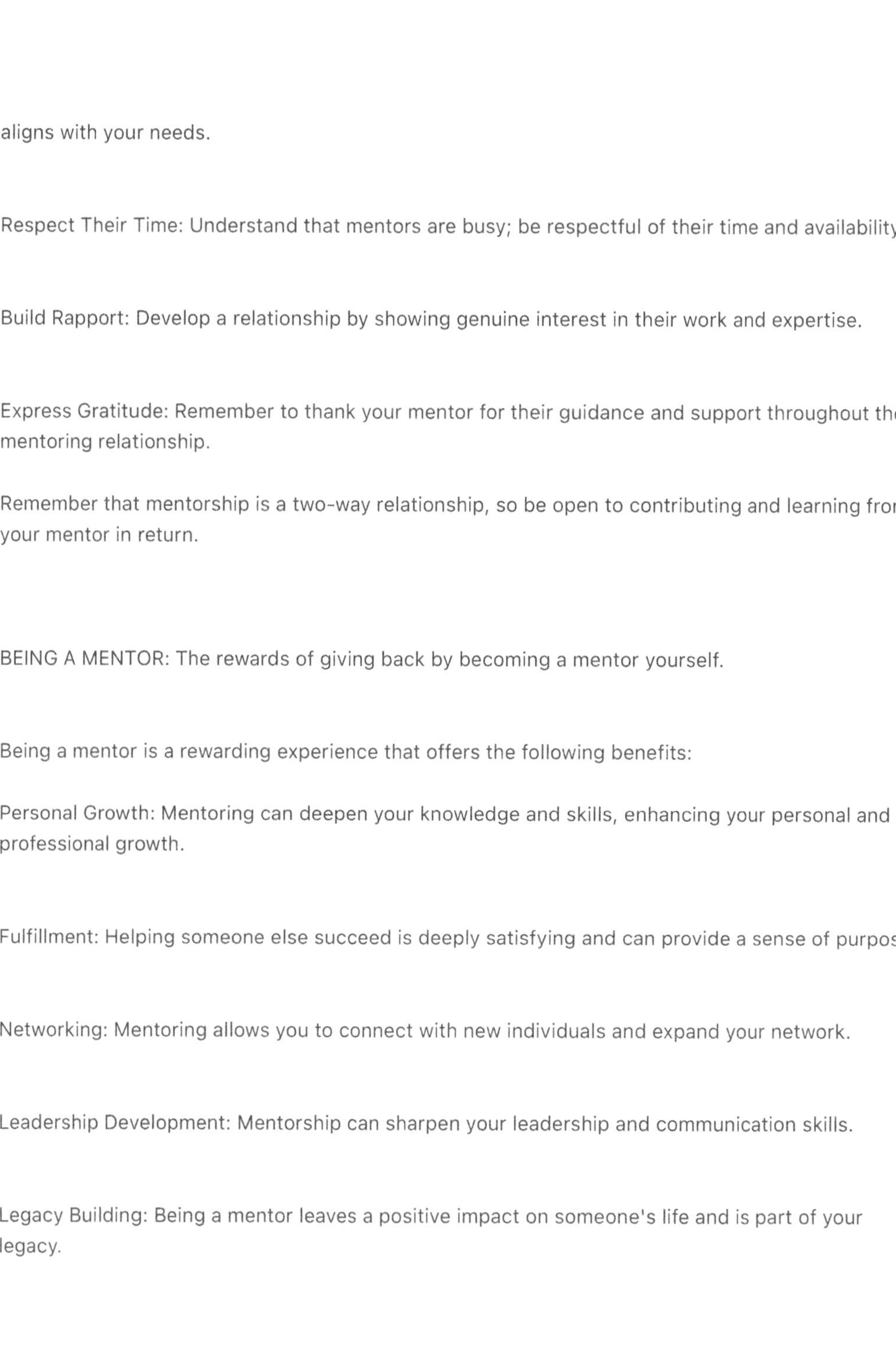

aligns with your needs.

Respect Their Time: Understand that mentors are busy; be respectful of their time and availability.

Build Rapport: Develop a relationship by showing genuine interest in their work and expertise.

Express Gratitude: Remember to thank your mentor for their guidance and support throughout the mentoring relationship.

Remember that mentorship is a two-way relationship, so be open to contributing and learning from your mentor in return.

BEING A MENTOR: The rewards of giving back by becoming a mentor yourself.

Being a mentor is a rewarding experience that offers the following benefits:

Personal Growth: Mentoring can deepen your knowledge and skills, enhancing your personal and professional growth.

Fulfillment: Helping someone else succeed is deeply satisfying and can provide a sense of purpose.

Networking: Mentoring allows you to connect with new individuals and expand your network.

Leadership Development: Mentorship can sharpen your leadership and communication skills.

Legacy Building: Being a mentor leaves a positive impact on someone's life and is part of your legacy.

Reciprocity: Mentoring can lead to meaningful relationships and support when you need guidance in the future.

COLLABORATION AND PARTNERSHIPS

COLLABORATIVE VENTURES: Exploring opportunities for partnerships and joint ventures in business and investments.

Collaborative ventures, such as partnerships and joint ventures, offer numerous advantages in business and investments, including risk sharing, resource pooling, access to complementary expertise, and the potential for accelerated growth and innovation. Careful planning and clear agreements are essential to ensure a successful and mutually beneficial collaboration.

SYNERGY IN FINANCE:

Synergy in finance is the idea that by working with others through a partnership, investment, or joint venture, a person or organization can achieve greater financial success than alone. Collaborative efforts often increase efficiency, share resources, and expand capabilities, ultimately improving financial performance.

DIVERSE PERSPECTIVES:

Working with people from different backgrounds and experiences can bring new perspectives and creativity to problem solving and decision making. It fosters innovation, enriches discussion, and helps uncover unique opportunities that ultimately lead to better outcomes in a variety of endeavors, including business, education, and community development.

FINANCIAL LITERACY FOR FUTURE GENERATIONS

TEACHING FINANCIAL RESPONSIBILITY

START EARLY :

In order to instill responsible money habits, it is very important to start financial education early. By teaching children the value of savings, budgeting, and money, they learn basic life skills that promote financial responsibility and security in adulthood.

PRACTICAL EDUCATION: Strategies for teaching kids about saving, budgeting, and investing.

Teaching kids about financial responsibility involves practical strategies:

Allowance: Give them an allowance to manage and save.

Budgeting: Encourage them to budget their money for spending, saving, and giving.

Savings Jar: Use a clear jar to show the progress of saving.

Piggy Bank: Teach the importance of setting aside money regularly.

Matching Contributions: Match a portion of their savings to incentivize them.

Financial Discussions: Engage in age-appropriate discussions about financial topics.

Investment Simulations: Show how investments grow over time.

Practical education empowers children to make informed financial decisions.

LEADING BY EXAMPLE: Modeling good financial habits for your children.

Setting an example and establishing good financial management habits is one of the most effective ways to teach children financial literacy. Demonstrating responsible practices such as budgeting, saving and buying helps them internalize these behaviors and apply them to their lives as they grow.

EMPOWERING THE NEXT GENERATION

SUPPORTING EDUCATION: Strategies for funding college and higher education for your children.

Supporting your child's education financially can be achieved through strategies like:

1)529 Plans: Invest in tax-advantaged college savings accounts.

2) Scholarships and Grants: Encourage academic achievement to secure scholarships and grants.

3) Financial Aid: Explore federal and state financial aid options.

4) Savings: Regularly contribute to dedicated education savings accounts.

5) Part-Time Work: Encourage your child to work part-time to help cover expenses.

6) Education Tax Credits: Utilize available tax credits for higher education expenses.

A combination of these approaches can help make higher education more affordable for your children.

INHERITANCE AND LEGACY PLANNING: Passing on financial wisdom and assets responsibly:

1)Estate Planning: Create a will or trust to specify how your assets will be distributed.

2) Communication: Talk to your heirs about your financial values, intentions, and the responsibilities of inheriting wealth.

3) Financial Education: Educate heirs about money management, investments, and financial responsibility.

4) Charitable Giving: Include philanthropy in your legacy, teaching the importance of giving back.

By combining these elements, you ensure a smooth transfer of assets while imparting financial wisdom to the next generation.

CHARITABLE GIVING:

Encouraging charitable giving within your family can instill a sense of social responsibility and compassion. Here is how to promote philanthropy:

1)Lead by Example: Show your commitment to giving back through your own charitable actions.

2) Discuss Values: Talk about the causes and issues that resonate with your family members and align with your family values.

3) Involve Children: Encourage children to participate in selecting charities and volunteer together as a family.

4) Create a Giving Plan: Establish a family giving plan that outlines your charitable goals, budget, and a timeline for contributions.

5) Research Charities: Investigate and choose reputable organizations that use donations

effectively.

6) Celebrate Acts of Giving: Acknowledge and celebrate the impact of your family's charitable contributions.

7) Matching Contributions: Consider matching family donations to magnify the impact.

8) Teach Financial Responsibility: Explain how budgeting for charitable giving is part of responsible financial management.

By integrating charitable giving into your family's values and practices, you foster a culture of generosity and create a positive impact on the causes you care about.

This chapter is developed to make you understand the importance of building a supportive financial community. You'll have insights into networking strategies to expand your professional and financial connections, the value of mentorship and collaboration, and how to pass on financial knowledge to future generations. This chapter empowers you to not only achieve your financial goals but also to contribute positively to the financial empowerment of others in your community and family.

CHAPTER NINF

STAYING UNSTOPPABLY RICH

INTRODUCTION

This last chapter is all about sustaining your financial empowerment and making it a lifelong journey. Building wealth is not a one-time achievement but a continuous process. In this chapter, we explore how to monitor and adjust your financial plan, celebrate your financial wins, and embrace a lifetime of financial empowerment.

MONITORING AND ADJUSTING YOUR FINANCIAL PLAN

THE IMPORTANCE OF REGULAR ASSESSMENT

FINANCIAL CHECK-INS: The significance of periodically reviewing your financial goals and progress.

Periodically reviewing your financial goals and progress through financial check-ins is essential for several reasons:

COURSE CORRECTION: It allows you to assess whether you're on track to meet your financial goals. If not, you can make necessary adjustments.

ADAPT TO LIFE CHANGES: Life circumstances change, and your financial goals should adapt too. Regular check-ins help you align your goals with your current situation.

BUDGETING AND SAVINGS: Tracking your progress ensures you stay disciplined with budgeting and saving, which is crucial for achieving your financial objectives.

MOTIVATION: Celebrating small wins along the way keeps you motivated and committed to your financial goals.

RISK MANAGEMENT: Regular reviews help identify potential financial risks or vulnerabilities, enabling you to take preventative measures.

INVESTMENT OPTIMIZATION: It allows you to reassess your investment portfolio and make adjustments as needed to maximize returns and manage risk.

In summary, financial check-ins provide the clarity, motivation, and adaptability needed to secure your financial future.

ADJUSTING FOR LIFE CHANGES: How life events like marriage, parenthood, or career shifts may require adjustments to your financial plan.

Life events such as marriage, parenthood, or career shifts often necessitate adjustments to your financial plan for the following reasons:

INCOME CHANGES: Marriage or career advancements can lead to increased income, while parenthood may reduce it due to childcare costs. Your budget must adapt accordingly.

NEW EXPENSES: Each of these life changes can introduce new expenses, like wedding costs, childcare, or home purchases, which need to be factored into your budget.

INSURANCE NEEDS: Marriage and parenthood often require adjustments in insurance coverage, such as life, health, or disability insurance to protect your loved ones.

ESTATE PLANNING: Parenthood may prompt you to create a will or trust to secure your child's future in case of unforeseen circumstances.

INVESTMENT STRATEGY: Career changes or life events may call for changes in your investment strategy to align with new financial goals or risk tolerance.

TAX IMPLICATIONS: These life events can impact your tax situation, influencing how you should file taxes and take advantage of credits or deductions.

In essence, adjusting your financial plan for life changes is crucial to ensure that your financial strategy remains relevant, efficient, and supportive of your evolving needs and goals.

EVALUATING INVESTMENT: Keeping an eye on your investment portfolio's performance and rebalancing as needed.

Evaluating your investment portfolio and rebalancing it as needed is crucial for several reasons:

PERFORMANCE MONITORING : Regular assessments help you track how your investments are performing relative to your financial goals.

RISK MANAGEMENT: Market fluctuations can skew your portfolio's risk profile. Rebalancing ensures it stays in line with your risk tolerance.

ASSET ALLOCATION: Over time, certain assets may outperform or underperform. Rebalancing helps maintain your desired asset allocation.

COST CONTROL: Rebalancing can minimize transaction costs and tax implications associated with holding onto poorly performing assets.

LONG-TERM OBJECTIVES: It aligns your investments with your long-term financial objectives and helps you avoid impulsive decisions based on short-term market movements.

DIVERSIFICATION: Rebalancing ensures that your portfolio remains diversified, spreading risk across different asset classes.

In essence, evaluating and rebalancing your investment portfolio is a proactive strategy to keep your investments on track and aligned with your financial goals, risk tolerance, and changing market conditions.

EMERGENCY PREPAREDNESS

Continuing to Build Your Emergency Fund: maintaining an emergency fund is crucial, even as you achieve your financial goals.

Insurance Review: Periodically reassessing your insurance coverage to ensure it aligns with your current needs.

Updating Estate Plans: Update wills, trusts, and power of attorney documents as circumstances change.

CELEBRATING YOUR FINANCIAL WINS

RECOGNIZING ACHIEVEMENTS

The Importance of Celebration: Celebrating financial milestones helps you to stay motivated and positive.

Setting New Goals: Try using your achievements as a springboard to set and pursue new financial goals.

Avoiding Lifestyle Inflation: Always be mindful of lifestyle creep as your income grows.

EMBRACING A LIFETIME OF FINANCIAL EMPOWERMENT

CONTINUAL LEARNING

Staying Informed: There is value in keeping up with financial news and trends.

Investing in Knowledge: Considering ongoing financial education and professional guidance.

Peer Networks: Explore the benefits of staying connected with your financial community for support and learning.

GIVING BACK

Philanthropy: Be ready to explore opportunities for charitable giving and making a positive impact on your community.

Mentorship: Paying it forward by becoming a mentor to others on their financial journeys.

Legacy Building: Always ensure that you plan for the legacy you want to leave behind for future generations.

I believe that in this concluding chapter, you'll have the knowledge and tools to maintain your financial empowerment for a lifetime. You'll understand the importance of regularly monitoring and adjusting your financial plan, celebrating your achievements, and continuing to learn and grow in the world of personal finance. This chapter not only helps you secure your financial future but also encourages you to give back and make a lasting impact on the financial well-being of others and the community.

CONCLUSION

YOU ARE UNSTOPPABLY RICH!

REFLECTING ON YOUR JOURNEY

Let us take a moment to reflect on the incredible journey you've embarked upon in "UNSTOPPABLY RICH: A Financial Guide for Women." Your journey to financial empowerment has been a transformational experience filled with insights, strategies, and empowering wisdom.

THE POWER OF FINANCIAL EMPOWERMENT

Financial empowerment is not just about amassing wealth; it's about taking control of your financial destiny, achieving your goals, and living life on your terms. Throughout this book, you've discovered the tools and knowledge needed to navigate the complex world of personal finance with confidence.

YOUR PERSONAL FINANCIAL LEGACY

As you conclude this book, it's important to recognize that you are now equipped to build and leave a financial legacy. Your financial decisions not only impact your own life but also the lives of those around you and future generations. By making informed choices, practicing responsible financial habits, and giving back to your community, you can create a positive and lasting impact.

EMBRACING LIFELONG LEARNING

Financial empowerment is a journey, not a destination. The world of finance is constantly evolving, and your financial goals may change over time. Embracing lifelong learning and staying adaptable are key to maintaining your financial empowerment.

STAY UNSTOPPABLY RICH

In closing, remember that being "UNSTOPPABLY RICH" goes beyond the numbers in your bank account. It's about the richness of experiences, relationships, and the positive influence you have on the world around you. You are the author of your financial story, and with the knowledge and confidence gained from this book, you can continue to shape a future that is truly unstoppable.

YOUR FINANCIAL JOURNEY CONTINUES

As you finish reading "UNSTOPPABLY RICH," your financial journey is just beginning or, if you've already started, it continues with renewed determination. The financial community you've built, the mentors you've found, and the wisdom you've gained will be your constant companions on this exciting and empowering path.

THANK YOU!

Finally, we extend our sincere gratitude for choosing "UNSTOPPABLY RICH" as your companion on this journey. We hope this book has empowered you to take control of your financial future, break through barriers, and become the unstoppable force you are destined to be.

Remember, you are "UNSTOPPABLY RICH" in potential, determination, and the ability to shape your financial destiny. The future is yours to conquer, one financial goal at a time.